teach
yourself

®

**keeping
aquarium fish**
dick mills

For UK order enquiries: please contact Bookpoint Ltd, 130 Milton Park, Abingdon, Oxon, OX14 4SB. Telephone: +44 (0) 1235 827720. Fax: +44 (0) 1235 400454. Lines are open 09.00–17.00, Monday to Saturday, with a 24-hour message answering service. Details about our titles and how to order are available at www.teachyourself.co.uk

For USA order enquiries: please contact McGraw-Hill Customer Services, PO Box 545, Blacklick, OH 43004-0545, USA. Telephone: 1-800-722-4726. Fax: 1-614-755-5645.

For Canada order enquiries: please contact McGraw-Hill Ryerson Ltd, 300 Water St, Whitby, Ontario, L1N 9B6, Canada. Telephone: 905 430 5000. Fax: 905 430 5020.

Long renowned as the authoritative source for self-guided learning – with more than 50 million copies sold worldwide – the **teach yourself** series includes over 500 titles in the fields of languages, crafts, hobbies, business, computing and education.

British Library Cataloguing in Publication Data: a catalogue record for this title is available from the British Library.

Library of Congress Catalog Card Number: on file.

First published in UK 2006 by Hodder Education, 338 Euston Road, London, NW1 3BH.

First published in US 2006 by The McGraw-Hill Companies, Inc.

This edition published 2006.

The **teach yourself** name is a registered trade mark of Hodder Headline.

Typeset by Transet Limited, Coventry, England.
Printed in Great Britain for Hodder Education, a division of Hodder Headline, 338 Euston Road, London, NW1 3BH, by Cox & Wyman Ltd, Reading, Berkshire.

The publisher has used its best endeavours to ensure that the URLs for external websites referred to in this book are correct and active at the time of going to press. However, the publisher and the author have no responsibility for the websites and can make no guarantee that a site will remain live or that the content will remain relevant, decent or appropriate.

Hodder Headline's policy is to use papers that are natural, renewable and recyclable products and made from wood grown in sustainable forests. The logging and manufacturing processes are expected to conform to the environmental regulations of the country of origin.

Impression number   10 9 8 7 6 5 4 3 2 1
Year   2010 2009 2008 2007 2006

contents

foreword

Keeping fish is unlike any other pet care you can envisage. Most companion animals (the latest politically-correct label to be attached to pets) provide a certain degree of interaction between themselves and their owners. Furthermore, they also share a capability to live, and perhaps survive without our aid, in our environment. Fish are not like that, as they live in a completely different world, one that we can only marvel at and only share by means of a suitable life-support system.

This factor alone means that we have to educate ourselves about fishes' way of life in order to provide adequate accommodation comforts for them. Then, the conditions of this environment must be maintained to the highest order for the fishes to thrive and, should their owner so desire, be persuaded to breed.

However, the outlook should not be regarded as a gloomy deterrent. Fish make excellent pets as the following list of advantages will show:

- Fishkeeping is literally a self-contained hobby and the fish make no inroads into our 'space'.
- They will not take over our favourite armchairs, bring home unwanted litters and need no late-night exercising.
- They certainly make no noise and, unlike cats, dogs and cagebirds do not become a 'tie' at holiday times as they can be left, unattended, to their own devices for up to two weeks.
- They are highly educational, as the fishkeeper will unconsciously encounter such topics as geography, mathematics, physics, chemistry, biology and genetics during their care. For families with children, here is an

excellent chance to teach the responsibility that comes with pet care; you'll even find that fishkeeping helps in answering those 'facts of life' questions that every parent has to face at one time or another!

Whilst ownership of an aquarium might seem to be an isolating interest, there is a large fraternity of fishkeepers that can be contacted within the many aquatic societies around the country. Several aquarium-related hobby periodicals are published monthly and there is no shortage of support from aquatic manufacturers' advisory services. On a wider scale, the Internet provides a more than convenient stepping stone to further information and aquarium contacts worldwide.

The main key to success is to understand the fundamentals of fishkeeping before you start; you must appreciate that a fish's life is not an area for experimentation whilst you find the best way to keep it. This is where this guide comes in.

There is a logical progression to the format of this book but you can also 'dip in' at any point to re-examine a particular subject.

There is a final bonus too: there is never any 'distance' between teacher and pupil – you are one and the same person, teaching and learning at your own convenient pace.

How to use this book

Just like any other 'instruction manual' this guide contains sections dealing with specific subjects, so you needn't read it from cover to cover if you don't want to. However, as we'll be eventually dealing with keeping living creatures, it is recommended that you regard the guide as a progression towards an actual target at the beginning; when you have grasped the basics, for instance, you can always come back and read any section more thoroughly if necessary.

So what's the strategy in planning a successful aquarium? Firstly, you've got to know what the fish requires in the way of a normal environment. Next, you'll not only learn how to provide that environment but also how to keep it at its best in the years to come, so that your fish have a long and happy life.

Any aquarium guide usually boasts a great visual selection of fish to whet your appetite, but you just can't keep anything and everything that appeals to you in the same tank. Compatibility either with its fellow tankmates, or with just being kept in captivity are two obstacles that you will have to overcome before your aquarium can bring you all the wondrous joys you are expecting of it.

It is no coincidence that real fish don't make much of an appearance until around halfway through this guide; up until then, they're much more theoretical but we make no apologies for this.

One problem with all newcomers to any hobby is their initial enthusiasm; they're desperate to get going. Unfortunately, the victim of this impatience is only too likely to be the very focus of your interest – in this case, the fish, which will undoubtedly suffer if you don't get things right.

Please bear in mind, fish can only bring their best to your home if you give them the optimum conditions and care. Don't forget to use this book well, before and during your fishkeeping – it's the least you can do for your fish!

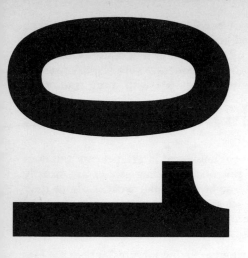

01

why keep fish?

In this chapter you will learn:
- the attractions of fish keeping
- the choices open to you
- at-a-glance comparisons.

Faced with a wide variety of suitable companion animals – cats, dogs and cagebirds immediately spring to mind – why should fish be considered? After all, they live in a completely different environment to ourselves and consequently need slightly more in the way of care than might be required with more traditional animals.

As attractive as cats and dogs might be, they do have some drawbacks which fish do not.

For a start, in order to prevent unwanted litters, pet cats and dogs (as opposed to pedigree potential breeding stock) are usually neutered early in life. Late-night exercising, worries about their welfare at holiday times to say nothing about noise, fur and feathers all over the place and the occupation of your favourite armchair are all the things that won't bother you with fish.

Aquariums are often described as 'living pictures' whose content is far superior to anything that television can bring; additionally, the fully-furnished aquarium can brighten up any dull, normally lifeless corner of the house, providing an interesting focal point at the same time.

With some exceptions (of which there are relatively few), most fish take kindly to captivity. The majority are hardy enough to adapt to the water that comes from the tap and, given good care and attention, should breed despite the odd bit of negligence on your part.

Modern day conservation concerns rightly question the practice of over-collecting fish from the wild. Many species of aquarium fish these days, however, wouldn't know their theoretical natural surroundings if they fell into them, as they are commercially bred in captivity many thousands of miles away from their native waters. An excellent selection is available at aquatic dealers around the country.

Aquarium equipment is totally reliable. You can build up your aquarium from separate components or buy a complete set-up including a furniture cabinet. A wealth of helpful advice is at hand from equipment and fish food manufacturers, local aquarium societies, hobby magazines and the Internet. There is simply no excuse for getting things wrong!

Based on these few facts alone, you have a hobby that is quiet, clean and unlikely to impinge too much on your daily life style. A few minutes maintenance each day and a couple of hours every fortnight or so is all that it takes to maintain an aquarium in optimum condition.

How will fishkeeping affect family life? You could not find a more family-suitable hobby – just consider the following subjects your children will encounter:

- Geography – where does that fish come from?
- Mathematics – how many litres/gallons in that tank?
- Chemistry – is that water hard or soft?
- Physics – what size heater will that new tank need?
- Biology – let fish help to explain the facts of life to your children.

The only real drawback – and you won't discover this until it is too late – is the amount of time you'll spend gazing into the aquarium's depths and admiring the activities of the brilliantly-coloured inmates.

The choice is yours

Thankfully, fishkeeping has long outgrown the 'goldfish in a bowl' level. Not only have we become more enlightened in understanding that fish deserve a better home, which technology has allowed us to do, but also modern day transportation systems mean that fishes captured or bred commercially abroad now arrive in dealers' shops in a far fitter condition, and far more likely to thrive in your aquarium. For the same reason, the number of species available is extremely wide. How you approach building up your own fish collection will be personal to you but the possibilities are almost endless:

- Will you go for a community collection of anything that takes your eye?
- Perhaps a 'biotope-correct' idea appeals with the focus on species from a particular geographic area?
- A singular group of fish may appeal – colourful livebearers perhaps or long-finned Siamese Fighting Fish?
- How about attempting to breed those species which have not yet been bred in captivity?
- On the conservation theme, why not set up a breeding programme to maintain endangered species?

There is also the attraction of watching fish get along with other animals and there are a couple of instances of this. The marine Clownfish, for instance, enjoys a very close relationship with the Sea Anemone in whose normally stinging tentacles it finds a safe haven. Then there's the freshwater Bitterling whose reproduction method includes the presence of the freshwater Mussel, without whom the fish could not breed.

There are numerous side avenues to explore too. You could easily get seduced by specializing in aquatic plants with fish forming only a minor proportion of your aquarium's interest. One popular 'side effect' of fishkeeping often rediscovered is photography; here's an opportunity for you to keep visual records of your aquatic prowess whether it be a favourite aquarium set up, favourite species or spawning sequences.

Before you begin to think that there are just too many alternatives to consider, study the following table which outlines the main attractions (and drawbacks) of fishkeeping's many areas of interest.

NOTE: The opposite table shows all of the possible areas of aquarium fishkeeping, however, given the limited size of this book we will concentrate on freshwater matters. Some aspects of marine aquarium management may not be discussed in great detail although many of the basic principles discussed will also apply to them.

Why choose a tropical freshwater aquarium?

In the same way that many people choose the most popular make of car, so fishkeepers tend to go with the common choice – the freshwater tropical aquarium (Colour Plate 1). The reason is simple: you get most for the amount of money you invest. The 'tropical' set-up is also very well marketed, with complete systems – heating, lighting and filtration all included – available ready to fill with water, decorate, and plug into the electricity supply and you're off almost immediately.

Another reason for the popularity of 'tropicals' is, as we will learn a little later, related to the number of fish any particular size of tank will support. As far as numbers go, this set-up is at the top of the numbers tree.

table 1 the possibilities of aquarium fishkeeping

what about	tropical		coldwater	
	freshwater	marine	freshwater	marine
ease of keeping	fairly easy	highly technical	moderately difficult	difficult
popularity	most popular	specialized	specialized	interest localized
availability of species	wide range of fishes in aquatic outlets	wide range of fishes in aquatic outlets	goldfish plus some limited native species	rockpool life
size of aquarium needed	modest sized	larger aquariums needed	larger aquariums needed	larger aquariums needed
breeding potential	easily bred	occasionally bred	easily bred	n/a
aquatic plants	yes	no, but macro-algae corals	yes	n/a
maintenance levels	low maintenance	high maintenance	low maintenance	high maintenance
support and help	plenty of support available – books, Internet, local societies	plenty of support available – books, Internet, local societies	plenty of support available – books, Internet, local societies	n/a

Despite the apparent technology involved, the tropical freshwater aquarium is probably as fool-proof and reliable as it can get. The heating system is fully automatic, the temperature of the water being thermostatically-controlled. The filtration system is easily maintained (assuming you understand what is needed), and fitting or replacing a fluorescent tube for the lighting couldn't be simpler.

When it comes to selecting fish for the tropical aquarium, again you're spoilt for choice, with a huge range of fishes from around the world to choose from. Within the species of fishes themselves, further choices offered are egg-laying or livebearing reproductive methods for those who wish to breed their own further supply of fish.

A supporting attraction is the underwater plants that can be cultured too. These plants, apart from their own intrinsic beauty have a much more important part to play in keeping water conditions healthy.

Why choose a coldwater freshwater aquarium?

Traditionalists might argue that if this area of fishkeeping was good enough for the Chinese nearly 2,000 years ago, there can't be much wrong with it. When you see what a huge hobby the culture of a single species fish has become in the succeeding years you have to concede they have a relevant viewpoint.

Yes, the coldwater aquarium is very much fixed around a single species, the Goldfish (*Carassius auratus*), (Colour Plate 2) but, of course, this single species has been aquarium-developed into many Fancy Varieties, many far removed from the original natural species.

It is interesting to note that the further removed from the original species the strains are, the less suitable they are for outdoor pond culture and more suitable for the indoor aquarium where their beauty can be seen much more conveniently!

You will not need any heating systems for a coldwater tank but, paradoxically, you may well need chilling equipment to prevent the aquarium overheating during summer!

One drawback, for some, is that a larger aquarium is required as the Goldfish (whatever variety) is much more oxygen consuming than other fish. Put it another way, fewer Goldfish can be kept in the same sized tank that would support many more 'tropicals'.

However, many strains of Goldfish can be enjoyed in an outdoor pond where an added attraction has to be the culture of colourful water lilies and other pondside plants but now we're veering towards water gardening rather than an indoor aquarium.

Why choose a marine tropical aquarium?

Anyone who has ventured beneath the waves over a coral reef whilst on holiday, or merely sat in front of a typical underwater world television programme will know the stupendous appeal of the multi-coloured fishes as they swim around the equally-colourful corals. The thought of creating such a scene in your own home cannot be denied.

For sheer pioneering thrills, this area of fishkeeping still offers excitement (and disappointments probably too) for those willing to take up the challenge.

Slightly more technical than freshwater 'tropicals' and, some would say, a whole lot more expensive, the marine tropical aquarium can be regarded as the pinnacle of achievement but it comes only as a reward for dedication and hard work in keeping the conditions at their very best at all times.

The aquatic plants of any freshwater aquarium are absent, but in their place come soft and hard corals and other invertebrate life such as shrimps and crabs.

Fish stocking levels are at their lowest in this area, so if it's number you want then you will need to find room for a huge aquarium plus its attendant filtration system.

Running costs are higher, mainly due to the regular need to buy salt mixes for replacement water changes. Many marine fish are comparable in price to their freshwater counterparts – as long as you don't get too ambitious!

Finally, whichever route you choose to take, remember there are no short-cuts to success, you've got to learn your trade first!

02

know your fish

In this chapter you will learn:
- the fish's basic design
- how colour is made and used
- the difference between fresh- and salt-water fishes.

Until you understand how a fish works as a living creature, you won't be able to comprehend the reasons for providing certain conditions for it as will be described in this book. Therefore, this section is not so much an identifier of individual species, but rather an insight into the fish's physical make-up.

Ask someone to draw a fish and you'll probably get the traditional fish shape but, if you've ever wandered into an aquarium shop or public aquarium, you won't need to be told that fish come in all shapes other than this. The reason is simple: fish come from all manner of waters – shallow and deep, fast flowing or stationary, warm or cold – and these differences in habitat have caused them to evolve into the different shapes and colours that so enthral us.

The basic design

Body and fins

Given that water is a rather incompressible medium, it follows that a fish's body ought to be of a design that lets it swim without too much effort. Hence most fish are of a tapered form from front to back.

Banks of muscles along the flanks sequentially build up, and finally transmit, power to the paddle-shaped tail fin at the rear that drives the fish forward through the water. The body is usually covered with scales or other bony plates. To ensure body flexibility, vital for the swimming process, scales are only fixed at their forward edges and are overlapped, tile-like, in the rearward direction; the slimy mucus covering the scales not only reduces friction between each scale but, of course, helps the fish to slip more smoothly through the water.

Although a fish's 'sliminess' may not appeal to many, it also serves an additional purpose in defending the fish against the effect of a parasitic or bacterial attack and in clothing an open wound. Often a fish's first response to changes in its environment might be to produce slightly more mucus as a precautionary measure.

To prevent the fish from undue rocking from side to side whilst on the move, the vertical dorsal and anal fins act as keels. Positional control is provided by two pairs of fins – the pectoral and pelvic fins. Pectoral fins, situated just behind the gills, make

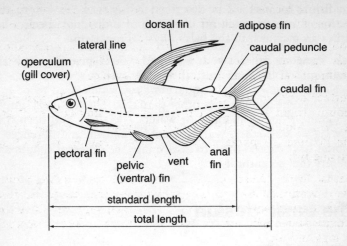

figure 1 a typical egg-laying species

manoeuvring easy, acting as brakes and/or hydroplanes in association with the pelvic fins under the body. Fins also play a large part in some fishes' reproductive behaviour. Males often court the female by 'strutting their stuff' and erecting their fins; female Corydoras Catfish, for instance, carry eggs between their pelvic fins to a spawning site. Egg-depositing Cichlids regularly fan their fertilized eggs to keep both oxygenated water flowing over them and also to prevent detritus settling on them.

You will certainly come across some fish – Tetras and Catfish, for instance – with an extra fin, the adipose, but the purpose of this is not clear.

The physical characteristic of fins can also be used as a guide to sexing fish. Male fish generally have longer, more pointed fins. In livebearing fishes, the shape of the anal fin is a clear indication of gender: the male's anal fin is rod-like, whilst the female's fin is fan-shaped (see Figure 29).

The position of the mouth can tell you a lot about a fish's life style. The gathering of food is an important factor to any fish and the position of the mouth will indicate where the fish tends to spend most of its time. Whisker-like growths around a fish's mouth are known as 'barbels'; these have taste buds which allow the fish to locate food in murky waters or darkness. Taste buds are also found on the long filament-like pelvic fins of Gouramies.

Top-mouthed species usually have flattish backs which shows they tend to inhabit the top layers of the water, grabbing floating foods such as insects from the surface.

Further down in the water, fishes having terminally-positioned mouths (right at the tip of the snout on a mid-line level) grab at their food as it falls through the water or, in the case of the Piranha, snapping chunks of flesh from the sides of any passing fish.

Catfish live on the substrate, so to facilitate feeding their mouths are downturned and act like a carpet-sweeper to gather food. Other Catfish, and some Cichlids, have rasping teeth inside such mouths which efficiently remove algae from sunken objects such as logs and rocks.

Gills and other special organs

Living under water means the fish has to extract oxygen dissolved in the water. Water is taken in through the mouth, passed over the delicate gill membranes and passed out via the gill openings on each side of the head. Whilst this is the standard method of respiration, some fish, such as Gouramies and Siamese Fighting Fish have an extra organ in the head that allows storage of atmospheric air gulped in at the water surface. This stands the fish in good stead should dissolved oxygen levels fall. Another respiratory aid can be found in some Catfishes who have the ability to store air in their hind-gut from where oxygen is extracted in times of need.

Fish don't have to worry about bobbing up to the water surface as an automatic buoyancy tank exists within their body. This is the swim-bladder that gives the fish neutral buoyancy, allowing it to rest at any level in the water that it chooses. Typical swim-bladder problems manifest themselves in the fish tumbling 'head-over-heels' or being unable to stay in mid-water. This is quite prevalent in many Fancy Goldfish whose body shapes have been modified by selective breeding to a designed shape with the result that the internal organs have become cramped and so malfunction.

Like us, fish have senses of sight, sense and smell, although the sense of smell (via nostrils) is unassociated with their respiration process. The sense of smell in some species is remarkably sensitive – one hears of Sharks being able to detect blood in the water from great distances.

Naturally, too, fish have a sense of touch. Whilst it is most practicable to use a net or jar to capture fish, handling large fish, such as Goldfish, is often unavoidable and wet hands should be used to avoid stressing the fish. This procedure will also limit the amount of mucus removed from the fish which otherwise would be rubbed off by 'dry' hands.

Whilst fish have eyes, their eyesight performance depends as much on the clarity of the water as on the efficiency of their sight-gathering organs. Fish with large eyes, such as the marine Squirrelfishes, *Myripristis* spp., are likely to be nocturnal by nature and need large, light-gathering eyes to locate their prey. Analogous to the size of puppies' paws, many fishkeepers think that any large-eyed freshwater fish, especially members of the Cyprinid family are likely to grow very big!

Fishes' eyes are controlled in a slightly different way to the human eye inasmuch as the focus is corrected by moving the whole eye forward or back, rather than altering its shape as is the case with our eyes. Naturally, fish do not have any need for eyelids to protect the eye or to keep it moist but some fish, such as Sharks, have a nictitating membrane – a kind of transparent eyelid – which protects the eye as the Shark moves in to attack its prey.

With no eyelids, fish can be sensitive to bright light: again, the Shark has a slit-like pupil which can be adjusted to limit the amount of light entering the eye, a ploy which is echoed in the *Hypostomus* freshwater Catfish which can extend or expand a fatty lobe of flesh across the eye to achieve the same light-limiting purpose.

So, fish have all the five senses that we have but, in their particular environment, they have an extra sense which comes in really useful in darkness or in murky water conditions. Look closely at a fish. Along its flanks you may be able to pick out a line of tiny holes, like a row of pin-pricks. These 'holes' are the entrances to an internal canal linked to pressure sensitive cells. This 'lateral line system' allows fish to detect changes in water pressure around its body allowing it to sense obstacles in its path or any other approaching fish.

Electricity is also used by some fish species as an additional 'sense'. Whilst the Electric Eel may use its ability to generate electricity for offensive purposes, stunning its prey for instance, other fishes use electricity for a much more benign reason. By generating an electric field around their bodies, and having the ability to sense variations in its reflected strength, fishes such as the Elephant Nose can navigate effortlessly in murky waters detecting obstructions and other fishes in the process.

Both of these last two 'senses' or capabilities are exclusive to fish and one can only imagine how useful they are when darkness falls or the water turns so murky that the use of sight is not possible.

It may come as a surprise to learn that fish can also hear. Hearing in fish is the subject of great technical depth and debate: their ears, for instance are not connected directly to the outside surrounding water, a set of bones, the Weberian Ossicles, is often used as connections to the swim-bladder to transmit sounds to the auditory system and so on. There is also the question of when does transmitted sound through water become a physical vibration that is perhaps more easily detected by the fish's other sensory systems? As a certain Star Trek commander might say 'Fish do have a hearing capability, but not as we know it.'

Colours and patterns

Colour, the very thing that attracts us to fish in the first place, also has more practical uses. It identifies the species (to others members of its genus, as well as to the fishkeeper) and may be used for camouflage, or other purposes.

The normal fish colouration is a dark dorsal (top) surface shading down to a lighter colour on the ventral (belly) surface. This suits the vast majority of fish as their main perceived extra-water predators are likely to attack from above the surface, and the dark top colouration will hide the fish against the dark background of the river or stream bed. From below, the light belly colours make the fish blend in with the lighter 'sky' colour, again making predatory attack (this time from within the water) less likely to succeed.

Of course there has to be exceptions to this rule and none more obvious than in the Upside Down Catfish, *Synodontis nigriventris*, which because of its perverse nature of swimming upside down has a dark coloured belly and a lighter coloured back.

You will notice too that these colours, or patterns, will vary as you look at your fish and become more attuned to their habits. Colours are often intensified or faded according to the mood of the fish, whether it's frightened for instance, or trying to attract a mate or threaten a rival. In general, male freshwater fish have the brighter colours.

Colour is produced in two ways – by pigmentation or by the laying up of light-reflecting waste materials (guanin) immediately below the skin. Changes in the colour pattern, for reasons as described above, are achieved by the fish expanding or contracting the pigmentation cells, known as chromatophores.

The brilliant electric-blue line of the Neon Tetra is produced by light being reflected back from guanin beneath the skin, the colour being determined by the angle of reflection. Goldfish can have three types of apparent colouration – metallic, nacreous and matt – again depending on how the guanin is located beneath the scales.

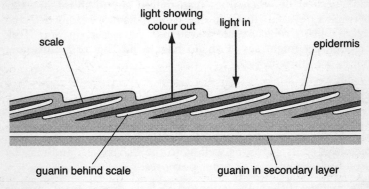

figure 2a the full 'metallic' look is due to guanin beneath every scale

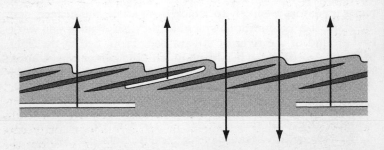

figure 2b 'nacreous' or a 'mother of pearl' effect is seen where only some of the scales are guanin-backed

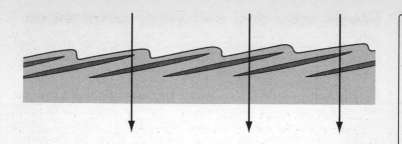

figure 2c 'matt' fish with no guanin beneath the skin appear to have a dull skin

Colour patterning is also used to provide decoy targets as a defence mechanism. For example, there are many fish that have dark 'eye'-spots in their fins or on their bodies well away from their actual eyes. Any approaching predator is faced with guessing which 'eye' is the real functioning organ; failure to injure this vital organ puts the advantage back with the intended victim who may well then escape unscathed or, in our fish world context, uneaten! Marine tropical fishes are prime examples in having decoy false eye-spots.

Colour helps to protect against predators too, for instance, if you don't look particularly like a target. Some marine fish feature deliberately disruptive colour patterns which either allows them to blend in with the background or, alternatively, interferes with their appearance by apparently breaking up their perceived 'fishy' outline. Of course, this works the other way round too, with some predatory fish using their cryptic patterning as camouflage as they lie in wait for any passing meal!

A remarkable use of 'spots' produced by colour patterning occurs in some African mouthbrooding Cichlids. During spawning, it is obviously important that the eggs be properly fertilized; to ensure that this is achieved, the female needs to pick up the male's sperm to fertilize the eggs which are then stored in her mouth.

The male's anal fin is decorated with 'egg-spots' and the female may nuzzle these in an attempt to pick them up along with the actual eggs laying on the substrate. In doing so, she stimulates the male into releasing sperm which she then draws into her mouth along with the eggs; efficient fertilisation is thus achieved. In other Cichlids, the male's sperm delivering ovipositor is often of a contrasting colour, again to entice the female to ensure correct fertilization occurs.

Freshwater and saltwater differences

With the technical advances made in recent years more and more people are able to keep the colourful tropical marine fish from the world's coral reefs.

Despite fishes from both freshwater and saltwater having similar outward appearances they work on opposite principles in some respects. You will learn that the two different areas of water, saltwater and freshwater, have a significant effect on the fishes' adaptability and thus on their subsequent care in captivity.

One major difference is how the internal workings of the fish deal with the differing type of water surrounding it. The fish's skin and gill membranes act as one-way valves allowing water to pass through it in one direction only. Where the fluids on each side of such a membrane are of differing 'strengths', according to the laws of osmosis, the tendency is for the less dense fluid to flow through towards the stronger.

As the marine fish is surrounded by salt water, a fluid more dense than that of the fish's internal fluids, water is continually passing out of the fish. To combat this, the marine fish literally 'drinks like a fish' to avoid dehydration and passes very small quantities of urine.

In freshwater, the scenario is reversed with water continually being absorbed into the fish. To prevent being constantly swollen with water, the freshwater fish needs to pass water out more often, and more copiously, than its marine counterpart.

With very few exceptions, such as the Eel and Salmon, it is unusual to find species that can traverse between the two types of water. However, juvenile forms of some fish such as Scats and Mono Angelfish are found in brackish water (half salt, half fresh) but migrate to full strength salt water as they mature into adults.

Use the evidence

By studying the shapes and forms of fish, and the differences in their natural life processes, before buying them, you can build up a list of requirements which will ensure you give them the best living conditions to suit their needs.

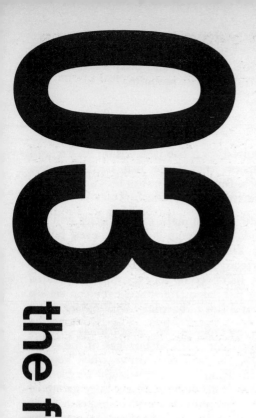

03

the fish's needs

In this chapter you will learn:
- how much space fishes need
- what fishes feed on
- how light is important.

Putting the obvious answer 'water' aside, fish are very much like any other living creature when it comes to basic needs. A fish needs **space** in which to live, **food** to build body materials and to supply energy, and **light** to act as a stimulus.

Space

The amount of space required for a fish depends on its size and it's a reasonable conclusion that large fish need a larger aquarium than tiny species. But the amount of space is not just to allow the fish adequate swimming room.

Fish are not necessarily sociable animals; many species will not tolerate other species and, in extreme cases, not even fellow members of their own kind or similarly-coloured fish to themselves. There is a perfectly natural reason for this – survival of the species – and many fish become very territorially-minded when breeding. By giving fish adequate space, each can set up its territorial boundaries and live in harmony with others.

On the other hand, many species are gregarious – think *Corydoras* Catfish (Colour Plate 30) and Loaches of the *Botia* genus (Colour Plate 32) – and will only thrive when kept in reasonable numbers. In aquarium terms, this might be from at least six upwards and there is no denying that a large group of fishes – Tetras or Danios – swimming together makes a great spectacle. Again, to accommodate shoaling species, the aquarium's physical dimensions must be more than adequate especially if you fancy keeping a shoal of large fish!

As will be explained later, a large aquarium will also allow more stable water conditions than those found in smaller volumes of water.

Food

In captivity, fish do not have the ability to seek out food as in nature. Every morsel has to be provided by the fishkeeper. Satisfying the appetites of a variety of species is quite an art. Not only has the diet of each species to be understood but also each species' individual feeding methods.

The average community collection of fish will contain fishes from a variety of waters – from fast-flowing to practically stationary. Fish also live at different depths in the water and so by combining these two factors it is clear that not all foods suit all fish and not all fish feed the same way, or at the same time of day.

Fishes can be omnivores, eating anything and everything, piscivores (which means that any bite-sized fish swimming by is at risk) or herbivores, favouring vegetarian matter in their diet. All these factors need to be considered. More information is contained in Chapter 12, which deals exclusively with feeding fish in captivity.

Fish that inhabit the upper levels of the water are adapted to take food from the surface and have up-turned mouths. The most suitable food for such fish is a flake-type food that floats for quite a long time, thus giving the fish every chance to eat.

Mid-water swimmers have forward facing mouths that snatch or bite food as it falls through the water: their food would be better to comprise of granule types that fall through the water a little faster than flake food; alternatively, freeze-dried food 'cubes' that can be stuck on the aquarium front glass at mid-water depth would also be an excellent way of presenting food to these fishes.

Catfishes, typical bottom-dwelling species, have downward-pointing mouths to assist in collecting food from the riverbed. Again a fast-sinking food would be best so that it escapes the attentions of fishes swimming above. Tablet and wafer-type foods fit these fishes' needs.

Fortunately, the fish food manufacturers have carried out intensive research both into what fishes need in terms of nutrition and how to simulate it commercially.

Finally, another consideration is not 'what?' or 'where?' fish eat but 'when?' Not all fish are active during daylight hours (or when the tank is illuminated) and many make their move at dusk and throughout the night. Keeping to a rigid daytime timetable of feeding will lead to these fish being neglected. Give some suitable, fast-sinking food just after 'lights out' for the benefit of nocturnal species. The problem of holiday feeding is addressed in Chapter 12.

Light

Without light we would not be able to see what is going on in the aquarium. Light is not just for our convenience as it provides stimulus for action by the fish and is also vitally important for any aquatic plant growth we may want in our aquarium. Water conditions are kept clean to a certain degree by the photosynthesis action of water plants.

As in all other areas of the hobby, the types of lighting and their fittings have been fully explored by specialist aquatic manufacturers and any lighting situation, from a tropical high noon in a jungle stream to a moonlight night on the coral reef, can be simulated in the aquarium.

By ensuring that these three important factors are taken into consideration, a big step along the road to success in keeping aquarium fishes will have been taken.

04

containing the interest

In this chapter you will learn:
- what size aquarium you will need
- how many fish you can keep
- how to choose the right aquarium.

Requirements

The container in which you keep your fish has to satisfy several prime requirements from our point of view for a start:

1 It must be watertight.
2 You must be able to see into it.
3 It must not rusty.
4 It ought to have a lid on it.
5 It should look nice.

BUT, more importantly from the fishes' point of view:

6 It must be big enough for the type and number of fish you intend to keep in it.

Points 1 to 3 are easily satisfied. All-glass (or, alternatively, acrylic) tanks are now the norm, replacing the old metal-framed, glass-stuck-in-with-putty models of yesteryear. It is equally fortuitous that modern tanks also make marine fishkeeping far more practicable, as they are much more resistant to the corrosive effect of salt water than earlier aquariums.

So sleek looking are the latest aquariums that any 'framing' used is there simply as decoration (or to give the fish some idea of where the boundaries of the tank lie) rather than as structural strengthening.

A lid is used for two main purposes: it acts as a covering to stop dust (and little fingers!) entering and fish jumping out, and also acts as a holder for any illumination that you wish to fit. There are, of course, instances where a cover (or hood, as it's usually called in fish circles) is not used and one instance of this is where high-powered pendant lights are used over an apparently 'open-topped' tank, although the tank does actually have a sheet of glass over it.

As most aquariums are set up in the lounge of a house, it should be an attractive addition to the existing 'furniture' rather than an eye-sore. Some 'picture shapes' look better than others – wide shallow tanks look too much like letterbox apertures, and tall narrow tanks are hard to plant and maintain – so don't go for anything over-fancy.

The weight of an aquarium

Many new fishkeepers fail to appreciate just how heavy a fully-furnished aquarium is likely to be.

table 2 the approximate weight and volume of a filled aquarium

---

approximate volume of water in a filled aquarium

60 × 38 × 30cm (24" × 15" × 12") = 15 Imp gall. = 62 l
90 × 38 × 30cm (36" × 15" × 12") = 24 Imp gall. = 102 l
120 × 38 × 30cm (48" × 15" × 12") = 31 Imp gall. = 136 l

approximate weight of a fully set up aquarium

60 × 38 × 30cm (24" × 15" × 12") = 186 lb = 83 kilos
90 × 38 × 30cm (36" × 15" × 12") = 275 lb = 125 kilos
120 × 38 × 30cm (48" × 15" × 12") = 430 lb = 192 kilos

Therefore, when buying an aquarium, also consider what you're going to stand it on: make sure any supporting stand is capable of dealing with the total weight – a spare bureau or unused sideboard space will not be suitable! This aspect is dealt with more fully in Chapter 12.

The size of an aquarium

Whilst the above recommendations contain both practical and aesthetic guidelines, these are of more concern to us than to the inmates of the aquarium.

The size of the aquarium obviously depends on what space you have in mind for it, but looking at things from a more technical viewpoint, you should understand that a large volume of water will retain its good water quality longer than an aquarium having a small volume.

Looking at the tropical aquarium, a good minimum size is a tank volume of around 20 gallons (90 litres) but, more importantly, the proportions of the aquarium should be considered.

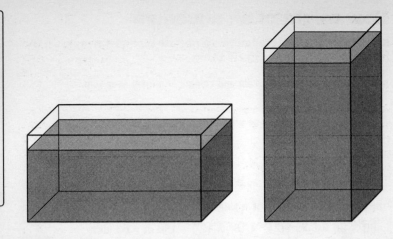

figure 3 tanks of identical volumes, different shapes

In the above illustration, both tanks are of the same 2 x 1 dimensional proportions and, will obviously hold the same amount of water and fish will have the same swimming space. Due to the fact that oxygen can only enter (and carbon dioxide leave) at the surface, the tank with the larger water surface area will support the larger number of fish. Therefore the tank on the left is a better choice from the 'fish-support' angle and is certainly much easier to service too.

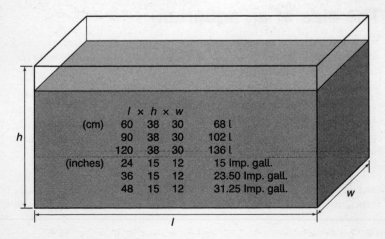

	l	$\times$ h	$\times$ w	
(cm)	60	38	30	68 l
	90	38	30	102 l
	120	38	30	136 l
(inches)	24	15	12	15 Imp. gall.
	36	15	12	23.50 Imp. gall.
	48	15	12	31.25 Imp. gall.

figure 4 approximate aquarium volumes

How many fish?

It is a natural assumption that the larger the aquarium, the more fish you can keep in it. Whilst this is obviously true, it is a statistic that can only be applied proportionately depending on what area of fishkeeping interest you intend to follow.

As observed earlier, it all depends on the oxygen levels in the water. Tropical aquarium water temperatures mean less oxygen than in coldwater tanks, and larger coldwater fish use up oxygen more than their relatively small tropical counterparts. Again, salt water contains a different amount of oxygen than freshwater. These factors conspire against the assumed conclusion.

In any aquarium, regardless of its actual dimensions and volume, you should understand that the maximum number of fishes kept is in this descending order: tropical freshwater, coldwater freshwater, tropical marine. The following illustration shows the typical maximums for a 90 cm × 38 cm × 30 cm (30in. × 15in. × 12 in.) tank.

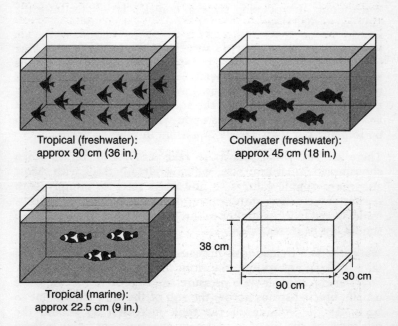

Tropical (freshwater):
approx 90 cm (36 in.)

Coldwater (freshwater):
approx 45 cm (18 in.)

Tropical (marine):
approx 22.5 cm (9 in.)

figure 5 the typical maximum number of fish recommended in a tank

Applying the guides:

- Tropical (freshwater) fish 30cm^2 per 1cm length of fish.
- Coldwater (freshwater) fish 60cm^2 per 1 cm length of fish.
- Tropical (marine) fish 120cm^2 per 1cm length of fish.

The comparative total fish stocks that can be held in each tank, depending on type of fish kept, are:

- Tropical (freshwater): 90 cm (36") total fish length.
- Coldwater (freshwater): 45 cm (18") total fish length.
- Tropical (marine): 22.5 cm (9") total fish length.

Incidentally, when measuring a fish, only measure the standard length (SL) from snout tip to end of body – don't include the tail.

For the newcomer to the hobby, there are excellent easy entry-level systems available from the aquatic dealer. Best described as 'fill up and go' aquariums, each comes complete with lighting and filtration systems and it really is a case of furnish the tank, fill up with water, plug into the electric supply and you're up and running. Introducing the fish comes a little later once the tank has settled down.

Having been made aware of these ready-made systems, you may think the rest of this book is superfluous. However, reading about the separate components – and their functions – that make up the whole aquarium form will not only give you a better understanding of how the aquarium actually works but it will also provide a firm basis upon which you may want to go on to plan your own, larger, aquarium in years to come.

There are also other factors to take into consideration when choosing an aquarium. Size, we have already dealt with. Most aquariums supplied for sale nowadays have to comply with certain construction standards and usually bear some kind of trade-agreed label or sticker to this effect. This is important and should not be disregarded.

Water exerts a tremendous pressure upon the glass walls of the tank. In long aquariums, the front and back panels can easily bow outwards under such pressure and to prevent this there are usually bracing straps across the top of the tank from front to back. As the volume of the tank increases, so should the thickness of the glass used in its construction; again agreed thickness recommendations are in place for aquariums made by reputable companies.

Small acrylic tanks are often aimed at the children's market but these are usually too small for long-term fishkeeping success.

The choice between glass and acrylic is a personal one, the main perceived drawback being that acrylic scratches more easily during cleaning. However, providing the correct cleaning pad is used, there should be minimal damage caused and acrylic's 'formed-all-in-one-process' does allow for some remarkable aquarium designs.

Although you should always choose the largest aquarium you can afford (for the sake of the fish, you understand), you should also ensure that it doesn't take up every inch of its allocated space – make sure that there is enough room around, above and beneath the aquarium for regular, trouble-free maintenance tasks.

05
it's a watery world

In this chapter you will learn:
- all about the world's water
- if your domestic water supply is suitable
- how to test water quality.

There is no denying that what any fish needs first and foremost is water. To us, water is something that's literally 'on tap' 24 hours a day and it serves our purposes extremely well whether it's for drinking, washing the car or bathing in. To a fish, it's something far more important – it's a complete living environment and needs to be understood if keeping fish is to be a successful hobby in your life.

The world's water

To get to grips with water and its complexities, take a look at some vital statistics:

- 77 per cent of the world's surface is covered by water (figure 6a).
- Only around 2 per cent is fresh water, the rest is salt water (figure 6b).

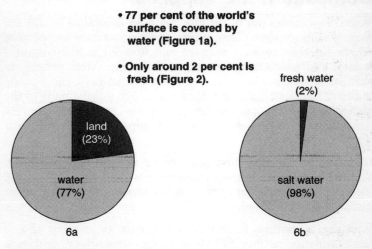

- 77 per cent of the world's surface is covered by water (Figure 1a).

- Only around 2 per cent is fresh (Figure 2).

figure 6 the Earth's surface

The latter statistic is vitally important when it comes to caring for fish, especially tropical marine fish. Conditions are so stable in a large body of water such as an ocean that the fish have little or no tolerance to changes in water quality like those that are likely to occur in captivity. Hence marine fishkeeping is considered more difficult, although it is the readiness of the fishkeeper to adhere to the discipline of maintaining strict water conditions that may be seen as the actual difficulty.

Despite the apparent minority proportion of fresh water – a fact hard to comprehend when rivers as large as the Amazon and the Nile are taken into consideration – the quality of fresh water can vary enormously from one geographic area to another. Mountain streams, jungle creeks, large lakes and huge rivers all contain fish which have adapted to the prevailing water conditions. This means that freshwater fish are adaptable and able to tolerate different conditions of water in captivity, so they are somewhat easier to keep, although the fishkeeper must not become complacent (or negligent) over maintenance.

We will concentrate on the management of water quality in freshwater aquariums in this chapter, although many of the facts and procedures described also apply to a certain degree to sea water too.

Domestic water supplies

Water, as it comes out of the tap, has been treated to be safe for human consumption. This means certain additives are present which fish are unlikely to have encountered in their natural habitat and which may adversely affect them. Most people are familiar with chlorine in this respect. Fortunately, the aquatic industry has come up with treatments which nullify many of the additives and so can make tap water more suitable for fishkeeping – something not always appreciated by the local water authorities!

In general, most aquarium fish offered for sale will survive in domestic tap water but for those species that are a little more 'delicate' the fishkeeper should know something of how water quality may be defined.

Basically, all natural fresh waters originate as rain but absorb 'contaminants' as they fall through the atmosphere, permeate through various soils or flow over differing substrates. These dissolved materials make the water either acid or alkaline, hard or soft.

Moving a fish from an environment with one particular quality of water into another too abruptly will cause it to become stressed and therefore liable to contract disease. A typical example of this is where you may buy a fish in an area using one supply of tap water and take it home where your supply is quite different.

The point was made earlier that freshwater fishes are fairly tolerant to change but this only holds good as long as the change is very gradual, so that the fish can be acclimatized to the new conditions as slowly as possible.

pH levels and water hardness

As there is insufficient space in this book to delve too deeply into the technical aspects of water we will concentrate in the two main parameters – pH and hardness – of freshwater quality.

Acidity and alkalinity form the two 'halves' of the pH scale.

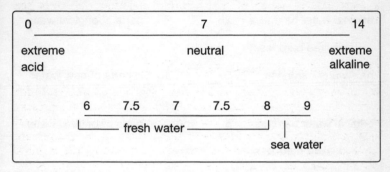

figure 7 where aquarium water fits into the pH scale

The whole range is numbered from 0 to 14: 0–7 is acid, 7–14 alkaline, with each unit being ten times the preceding one. For example, a pH of 8 is ten times more alkaline than pH of 7; and so a pH of 7 is ten times more acid than pH of 8. In the natural swing of things, the pH range that concerns us as fishkeepers covers between 6.5 and 8.2, while not a huge difference on the face of it, it is in fact almost a 100-fold difference from one end to another.

Fish from jungle streams generally prefer acidic water as their natural home is full of fallen vegetation which decomposes in the water to give an acidic reaction. Alkaline waters usually turn out to be harder in nature. Jungle waters are likely to be soft, with few dissolved minerals. Central American fish, such as the popular livebearers are found in more alkaline waters as are fishes in Africa's Rift Valley Lakes, which are just enormous water-filled rocky clefts.

Turning back to domestic supplies, the quality of water from the tap depends on the water's source which may be many miles away from its eventual distribution point. Water from mountains and lakes is likely to be soft whilst water draining off chalky soils will be much harder.

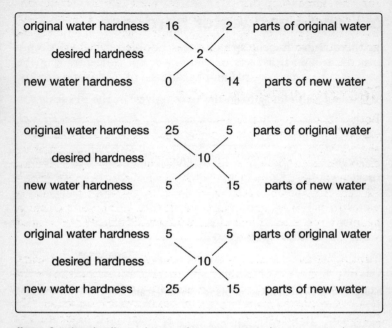

figure 8 using the diagonal proportions as an example, you can work out how much new water (of a different hardness) to add to existing water to adjust hardness to value required

Altering the condition of water is not too difficult in respect of 'hardness'; simply diluting hard water with a quantity of known softer water (clear rainwater for instance) will bring down the overall hardness quite easily. Should it be necessary to harden the water more, then using a calcareous (calcium-rich) substrate will do the job gradually without killing the fish in the process. Changing the pH is slightly more difficult, as the degree of water's inbuilt resistance to pH changes (known as buffering) will obviously vary due to differing basic water qualities from locality to locality, but it can be done. You must ensure that all changes to water quality are made as gradually and over as long a period as possible to avoid stressing the fish.

Within this book, the importance of researching any fish's needs before buying it will be reiterated many times. However, you can be caught out as many fish are commercially-bred thousands of miles away from their original, natural habitats. In these cases, the water requirements for the wild fish may not be the same as for the same fish that have been bred for the aquarium. Furthermore, the water parameters at your dealer's premises are likely to be different again – so, whilst research is all well and good you have to be aware of these possible anomalies.

Testing water quality

Both the pH and hardness parameters can be checked very easily. The relevant Test Kits are available at all aquatic retail shops. Most Test Kits use liquid reagents (although in some cases the use of solid pill reagents might be needed) which are used in conjunction with the supplied colour comparator charts. All that is involved is adding the necessary reagent to a phial of water to be tested and comparing the resulting colour change against a reference colour chart which will indicate the relevant value (see also Chapter 09).

Turning to the marine aquarium, where maintenance of water quality is paramount, there is another characteristic to be considered. The majority of aquarium water used for marine tanks is synthetic sea water rather than natural sea water. The fishkeeper uses bags of 'salt mix' to prepare the water and, to ensure that this is of the correct 'strength,' its specific gravity (SG) needs to be checked (see Chapter 09). This is done using a hydrometer and the average SG value is 1.020, against the normal natural sea water value of 1.023. Because the SG value varies with temperature, it is important to use a hydrometer suitable for marine aquarium use, as it will have been calibrated for use at the correct water temperature.

This extra discipline (and expense!) is exclusive to marine fishkeeping, as new sea water must be mixed each time to replace that removed when carrying out regular partial water changes. Changing the SG value is simplicity itself: if it is too low, add more salt mix; if too high, add more fresh water. These changes should always be made outside of the aquarium. Never add salt mix directly to the aquarium.

The management of water conditions is vital to success. With correct attention, fish will thrive and almost certainly breed, providing you give them the correct living environment.

06 the hardware store

In this chapter you will learn:
- heating the aquarium
- aquarium lighting
- filtration systems.

Fish will not thrive in captivity unless we are able to replicate, as closely as possible, the conditions they enjoy in nature. Fortunately for us, the aquarium manufacturing industry has risen to the challenge admirably providing reliable, efficient equipment for the task in hand.

Apart from 'food' which will be considered in a separate section, there are four main areas to discuss here – **heating**, **lighting**, **filtration** and **aeration**.

Heating

Attempting to keep tropical fish in a more temperate zone than that from which they originate will mean that their aquarium water will need heating and and maintaining at a specific water temperature. Keeping this temperature constant is not difficult and it needn't be exactly 'constant' all of the time as even in the tropics there are natural temperature fluctuations between daytime and night-time. But won't it cost a lot of money? Let's take a closer look at what is involved in keeping the aquarium at the right temperature.

The aquarium is like a storage heater and once it reaches the required temperature then very little energy is needed to keep it there. During winter months, when our homes are centrally heated, in the cosy warmth of the lounge (or whatever room you keep the tank in) little energy will be needed to maintain the desired heat level in the aquarium. The following diagram shows what's happening in a simplified way.

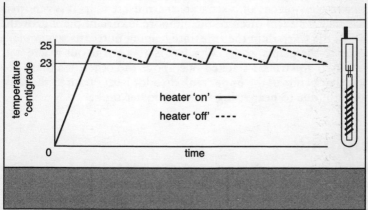

figure 9 operating principle of thermostatically-controlled heater

The initial heating of the tank water uses the most energy. After that, all the heater unit has to do is keep the temperature 'topped up.' It switches off when the set temperature is reached and comes on again after a certain heat loss has occurred – all done automatically by the thermostat unit combined with the heater. So what is there to worry about?

You should tailor the size of the heater to the size of the aquarium. Fitting a small heater to a large aquarium means that the heater will be switched on quite a lot and the tank will take a long time to heat up over its entire length. In the old days of electro-mechanical thermostats this prolonged 'on' period could mean damage to the thermostat contacts. Fitting a large heater to a small tank leaves no margin for safety should the thermostat decide to stick 'on' – the small quantity of water would soon over-heat severely with drastic consequences to the fish. The smell of 'boiled fish' is something you never forget!

Our suggested size tank, 600 mm tank (24" long) by say 38 mm (15") deep, will generally only need a 150 watt heater if the tank is housed in a normally furnished and heated lounge.

There are alternative forms of heating for the tropical aquarium other than having a thermostat/heater unit in the tank. Some large outside power filters can have heating units built into their design but, due to some exposed metals in their construction, may only be suitable for freshwater tanks unless a marine use is specified too.

Another alternative form is the undergravel heating system. Here, a heating cable is buried under the substrate; temperature control is by means of a separate thermostat unit. It is reported that such a system often results in more luxuriant plant growth, due to the warmth in the substrate helping nutrients to circulate better to the plants' roots. This fact is also borne out where you have two aquariums stacked one above the other; it's often the case that plants in the upper tank do a lot better than in the tank beneath, due to heat rising from the lower tank.

Lighting

Lighting is essential as it stimulates all life and, of course, we want to be able to see into the aquarium.

The usual light source for aquariums is fluorescent tube. Although traditional tungsten lamps (now thought outdated and inefficient) still work and have their adherents, they produce too much heat within the aquarium hood which, in turn, often shortens the life of such lamps.

The lighting fitted 'as standard' is adequate for fish-watching but an increase in light intensity will be needed for better plant growth in freshwater tanks and coral growth in marine aquariums. Fit more tubes, if there is room in the hood, or make better use of the light you have already got by fitting clip-on light-enhancing reflectors to the tube.

However much light you have, it won't do any good if it doesn't penetrate down into the aquarium. Keep the cover glass clean! Murky water will also cut down the beneficial light so make sure a filtration system is not only fitted but also maintained regularly.

You can buy different fluorescent tubes for different purposes: to enhance colours of the fish or to encourage better plant growth for instance.

Modern 'luminaires' – fittings which clip on to each side of the aquarium – do away with the traditional aquarium hood. These can be fitted with normal-sized fluorescent T8 tubes or the latest slimmer (and brighter) T5 tubes.

High-intensity metal halide lamps (housed in a pendant fitting) over an open-topped tank are best for large, deep tanks. You will still need a cover glass to prevent damage to the lamps from water splashes.

Keep the lights on for around 10–12 hours each day, as this is what the fish get in nature.

Too much light will result in rampant algae growth. Cut down the amount of light (either intensity and/or duration), plant more plants or introduce some algae-eating fish!

Lamps do not last forever, a fact easy to ignore. Renewing fluorescent tubes every year will ensure that your aquarium never loses its visual appeal.

Filtration

Ask most intending fishkeepers what they think a filter's primary function is and the answer will be 'to keep the water clear'. This is an understandable reply, but it's not the whole story as even the clearest water can be quite unsuitable for fishkeeping.

Do we actually need filtration in the aquarium? To the fish, living in the aquarium is not like living in nature, where natural water flows clean the rivers or where the fish have the option to swim away from bad conditions should they so wish.

We have seen how water can be 'contaminated' by falling through the atmosphere or by what it flows through, or over. Many contaminants are invisible, being dissolved in the water. Then there's the effect on water just by having things living in it, or put into it, by the fishkeeper. All of these adverse effects on the water's quality can be nullified by the use of filtration.

Filtration works on three levels – *mechanical*, *chemical* and *biological* – all of which take place in the aquarium, depending on what equipment we install.

Water clarity is achieved by two of the above methods – mechanical and chemical filtration. The first works by using sponge or 'floss' material to simply strain out visible, suspended matter debris from the water. A more refined process takes place in reverse osmosis units where a special membrane, rather than a sponge or floss, removes many heavy metals and other undesirable elements in the water.

Chemical filtration uses activated carbon to take the discolouration out of water but it does it in a slightly different manner than by straining it out; in this instance, materials adhere (actually, adsorb) to the surface of each carbon atom. The carbon should be renewed regularly to avoid the risk of materials being dumped back into the aquarium water. Other unwanted materials in the water, such as nitrates and phosphates (both will encourage algae), can also be removed by using the appropriate filter media.

Types of filter

Filtration units can be used both inside and outside the aquarium. The most popular design is an internal unit, which includes a built-in electric water pump. There is usually a pre-formed sponge filter medium and often an option for using other types of filter medium such as carbon. Such units are available tailored in size to suit several set sizes of aquariums.

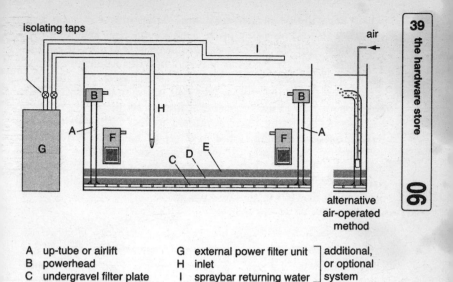

A up-tube or airlift
B powerhead
C undergravel filter plate
D gravel protecting mesh
E substrate
F internal power filter

G external power filter unit ⎤ additional,
H inlet   ⎥ or optional
I spraybar returning water ⎦ system

figure 10 filtration system variations

For larger aquariums, or where there is room under or near the aquarium, the so-called canister 'power filter' is a larger external unit which is connected to the aquarium by flexible hoses through which water is delivered to the filter and pumped back again after passing through the filter.

A natural form of filtration

Living animals produce waste material, plants die, fishkeepers over-feed – all truisms in the aquarium. The decomposition process of any of the above uses up oxygen and also produces toxic materials. We need to be able to remove these or convert them into less harmful substances.

We can encourage bacteria to work in our favour and this additional, alternative form of filtration is known as biological filtration.

There are millions of bacteria living on the surface of every grain of substrate and on every piece of rockwork that need to be fed. Fortunately for the fishkeeper, the bacteria feed on the primary products of decomposition – just what the aquarium doesn't need. The decomposition products are based on ammonia, something also expelled from the gills of the fish. *Nitrosomonas*, the first of two kinds of bacteria, known as nitrifying bacteria, set about converting toxic ammonia to less toxic nitrite. Once nitrite become available, the next set of bacteria, *Nitrobacter*, convert this to nitrate, an even less toxic substance, some of which can be used as food by aquarium plants. These useful bacteria work under oxygen-rich conditions, hence the need to keep them in well-oxygenated water.

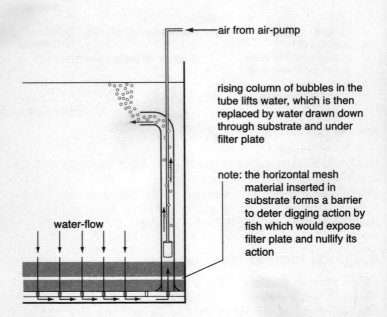

air from air-pump

rising column of bubbles in the tube lifts water, which is then replaced by water drawn down through substrate and under filter plate

note: the horizontal mesh material inserted in substrate forms a barrier to deter digging action by fish which would expose filter plate and nullify its action

water-flow

figure 11 how airlift works with biological filtration

An undergravel (biological) filter fitted beneath the substrate pulls oxygen-rich water through the substrate to maintain the bacteria colonies. Never switch off this filter for any appreciable length of time, as the bacteria will start to die off and take some time to re-establish themselves.

A development on this form of filtration is the 'fluidized bed' filter. Here, rather than pass water through a bed of substrate within the aquarium, a body of fine silica sand is held in an external tubular unit through which water is passed. As the sand is kept in constant suspension by the water-flow, there are millions of sites for nitrifying bacteria to colonize and the design is said to be far more efficient than previous biological filters.

All biological filters deplete oxygen levels in the water. Wherever possible, water returning from any biological filter should be aerated as it returns to the main body of the aquarium.

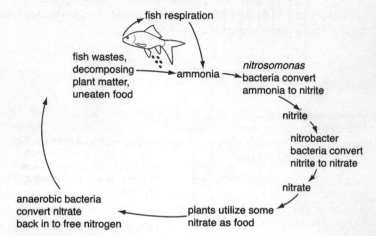

figure 12 the nitrogen cycle

Although most freshwater aquariums work well with these three levels of filtration, it is possible to take things a bit further to complete the natural 'nitrogen cycle' rather than stop at the nitrate stage. You can reduce the level of nitrates too by using yet more bacteria, the anaerobic denitrifying kind. These can be set up in a special filter to re-convert nitrate back to atmospheric nitrogen again but this is a tricky process which requires some expert handling to achieve successfully.

Marine fishkeepers have specialized filtration systems (protein skimmers) that remove organic compounds before decomposition sets in. The skimmer works on the theory that organic compounds are attracted to any water/atmosphere interface: a column of concentrated air bubbles, laden with organic matter attracted out of the aquarium water as it passes through, overflows into a collecting cup from where it can be periodically discarded. This process is also known as 'foam-fractionation'.

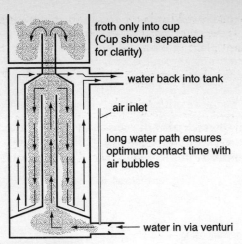

froth only into cup
(Cup shown separated
for clarity)

water back into tank

air inlet

long water path ensures
optimum contact time with
air bubbles

water in via venturi

figure 13 a protein skimmer

If used in conjunction with a protein skimmer, bacteria living on and within living rock deal with any remnants of organic manner in the usual biological manner described earlier and also complete the nitrogen cycle.

In addition to biological filtration, nitrate levels in freshwater aquarium can be reduced quite simply by carrying out regular partial water changes, as this process dilutes the build-up of nitrates produced.

Aeration

At one time, no aquarium was complete without a curtain of bubbles rising from behind a rocky outcrop or from a model diver or sunken treasure chest. All that was needed to produce this effect was a small air-pump, a length of neoprene tubing and a suitable airstone. Apart from being an active visual feature, the introduction of air into the aquarium – aeration – brought other benefits. Contrary to popular belief, the aeration bubbles do not introduce extra oxygen into the water directly; they actually agitate the water surface and encourage the natural ingress of atmospheric oxygen whilst at the same time allowing carbon dioxide to be expelled.

With every silver lining, there is bound to be an associated cloud: over-vigorous aeration can have an adverse effect on plant growth, as it can reduce the levels of carbon dioxide in the water that plants would otherwise use for photosynthesis and growth. This is the reason that carbon injection systems are used where luxuriant plant growth is desired.

With the introduction of filtration systems, the air-pump was also used to drive the early units which were either an internal plastic container filled with filter floss or external 'hang-on' units. Some undergravel biological filtration systems still depend on an air supply for their continuous water-flow, although electrically powered pumps can be used for this, so the air-pump is not quite relegated to the redundant equipment pile just yet.

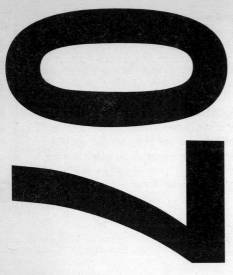

07

the green world

In this chapter you will learn:
- how plants benefit the aquarium
- some plant facts
- about various types of plants.

The benefit of plants

Aquarium plants serve several purposes, they are not there just to make the aquarium look nice. Except for a few instances, every aquarium will benefit by having them. Let's see what plants can offer from a fish's point of view.

In the natural world, where every animal forms part of an overall food chain, a nearby clump of aquarium plants provides a safe sanctuary if you're fleeing from the very real prospect of becoming some other fish's lunch. But, of course, this works the other way round with many an aquatic predator lurking in the aquatic plants ready to ambush a passing meal.

Apart from providing safety retreats, plants also offer natural resting places where a fish can get away from it all if it so desires and this certainly applies to those nocturnal species that like to keep a low profile during daylight hours before venturing out as darkness falls.

Plants can also harbour plenty of microscopic aquatic life and fish can spend many a happy hour browsing amongst fine-leaved plants for such tiny titbits. However, plants don't have it all their own way, as there are a number of species of fish that are decidedly vegetarian-minded when it comes to food and will avidly nibble at any green shoot that dares to push its head above the substrate.

Fish also make use of plants when breeding. Broad, stiff-leaved plants provide excellent spawning sites on which eggs can be laid; a dense bunch of fine-leaved plants can hide hundreds of scattered fertilized eggs during a spawning session, becoming a very effective prevention against egg-eating either by the parents or other fishes. Similarly, any newly-born fry will find such dense growths equally useful. Literally, plant material can be used constructively by fish when breeding: Gouramies often include bits of floating plant when building their bubble-nests, a practice also carried out by the coldwater Stickleback as it builds a tunnel of plant bits on the substrate in which to spawn.

To quite a great extent, plants act as water purifiers. Under the influence of the aquarium lights they photosynthesize and remove the carbon dioxide they need to build food for themselves from the water. As a by-product of this process surplus oxygen is released, giving rise to the name of 'oxygenators' to some groups of plants. It should be noted that this process is reversed during the hours of darkness, with carbon dioxide being released and oxygen consumed.

Plants may also take up nitrates to some degree, again helping maintain favourable water conditions in the aquarium.

Using plants

It's time to be selfish, as we're going to think about planting from our point of view, not that of the fishes – a not unreasonable attitude to take seeing as we'll be the ones looking at the plants from our side of the aquarium's front glass.

We use aquatic plants, along with other 'decorations', to disguise the tank's bareness and, of course they provide the fish with a sense of security. A planting plan suggestion can be found in Chapter 09.

Plant facts

Aquatic plants are not all the same; some require more light than others, some grow faster too. Unlike terrestrial plants, aquatic plants 'feed' through their leaves, absorbing nutrients direct from the surrounding water rather than through their root systems that are used mainly to anchor the plant in place.

Quite a few plants used in the aquarium are actually bog plants whose natural habitats are only covered in water at certain periods of the year; in between times, the plants grow in the moist or muddy soil only becoming completely submerged when the next rainy season comes to flood the area. It is normal for such plants to have differing leaf shapes under these different growing conditions. This is the reason why many aquarium plants lose their leaves when introduced into the aquarium – they're just readjusting their lifestyle to cope with the new condition. It also proves that they were initially grown commercially out of water.

Many species of plants are not only cosmopolitan but also have related species that are suitable for tropical and coldwater conditions. However, you should always try to choose the correct species for the water temperature of your aquarium; for example, coldwater species often 'run away' under tropical conditions.

Most plants propagate vegetatively, by sending out runners, new shoots that can be re-planted to provide extra greenery in the aquarium. A few species such as the *Aponogeton* genus have flowers above the water surface that can be pollinated to provide fertile seeds which can be planted in the substrate to grow into more plants.

If you want to use plants that prefer low light levels, then plant these under taller, faster-growing plants whose leaves float across the water surface and provide the required shade. Shade-loving plants include *Cryptocoryne* and *Anubias*.

Fine-leaved plants such as *Cabomba* and *Myriophyllum* enjoy bright light if they are not to become 'leggy' as they reach up in search of the light levels they require.

Plants do have one drawback – it's easy to introduce snails into the aquarium unwittingly due to snail eggs hitching a ride on the underside of plant leaves. Always inspect any new plants for snails' eggs – and remove the jelly-like blobs – before putting the plants into the aquarium.

Types of plants

You will find aquarium plants are often described as being of one of three types – 'rooted,' 'floating' or 'cuttings'. These groups have been created by fishkeepers for convenience, rather than by scientific groupings:

- **Rooted plants** are those plants having an obvious root system on top of which is a stem or leaves, with a distinct junction being the two sections. The leaf structure of rooted plants can be quite diverse – grass-like, oval, multi-branched or perforated – which allows for plenty of creative freedom when furnishing the aquarium. Typically, the broad-leaved Amazon Swordplant, *Echinodorus* sp., is often used as a specimen plant whereas the grass-like *Vallisneria* and *Sagittaria* are used as background plants.

- **Floating plants** are the free spirits of the plant world, the go wherever the water flow takes them. Generally small in size, they provide effective shade for the fish and those species, such as *Salvinia*, having long trailing roots hanging down into the water which make excellent refuges for baby fish. Perhaps their one drawback is that due to their natural position being on the surface, their close proximity to the aquarium lights tends to make them rampant growers! The ubiquitous Duckweed, *Lemna* sp., often finds its way into the aquarium as a stowaway on other plant leaves; this is another reason to rinse off and inspect any new plant introductions, unless you want a full-time job forever netting the Duckweed from the aquarium's water surface in the coming years!

- **Cuttings** aren't found in nature. As their name suggests, they are by-products of the fishkeeper's pruning activities; pieces cut from many plants (even severed leaves) will develop into more adult plants if re-rooted in the substrate. Favourite plants for providing cuttings include Water Wisteria (*Synemma*), *Hygrophila*, *Cabomba*, *Myriophyllum*, *Ambulia* and most other fine-leaved species.

Not quite the real thing

You may notice plastic replica plants for sale. These can serve a purpose where vegetarian-minded fish are to be kept. They will look reasonably realistic and offer all the advantages of real plants except they won't purify the water or provide a food source. Any algae that grows on them can be removed by scrubbing.

08

sticks and stones

In this chapter you will learn:
- about decorating the aquarium
- how to use wood
- arranging rockwork.

Despite the previous chapter, the underwater scene is not all green aquatic plants. All along their length, rivers are filled with fallen trees and dislodged boulders, their beds covered with scoured out sands. About the only things not found to any great extent in nature are those treasure chests, sunken galleons and mermaids.

With reference to Chapter 05 which dealt with water quality, you must be very careful as to what you put into the aquarium by way of decorative materials. This is particularly important if you wish to set up, and maintain, very strict water qualities for breeding, for instance, as anything that alters carefully set up water conditions will frustrate any attempt to keep and breed 'soft water' fishes such as Tetras and Discus.

Wood

The dark brown richness of a piece of bogwood or a branch to simulate a submerged tree root adds beauty and naturalness to the aquarium. It sets off the colours of the fish superbly and many fishes like resting amongst the branches or browsing on the surface of the wood.

You should use wood that has been dead for a long time, preferably a piece that is well water-logged too. Newer pieces of wood will produce mouldy growths or fungus when submerged and probably pollute the aquarium in the process.

Prior to use in the aquarium, all pieces of wood should be left in water (weighed down if necessary) for several weeks, changing the water regularly in the process. This will remove much of the dark tannins in the wood that would otherwise stain the aquarium water within hours of the wood being used. A possible alternative is to use several coats of polyurethane varnish on the wood but this can lift off after a while, especially if there is a slight gap in the coatings which allows water to get in.

You can cheat, of course, by using replicas of sunken logs that are made from safe resin materials using moulds taken from real logs. These are indistinguishable from the real thing after a few weeks in the aquarium.

Rockwork

Be careful with rockwork – you should ensure that the rock material is safe for prolonged use under water. It should not be soluble or contain any metal ores as either of these will alter the water chemistry, for instance, calcareous rocks will make the water harder. Notorious for hardening water are the plastercast model 'walls' and 'balustrades', which are, for some reason, aquarium ornaments favoured by many.

However, there is one excellent example where rocks will be welcomed in the aquarium – in an aquarium based on the conditions found in the African Rift Valley Lakes. Here, the endemic fish, mainly Cichlids, browse on the algae-covered rocks (the only 'plant material' around) and the natural water condition is extremely 'hard' because of the high level of mineral content in the water. Secondly, rocks can be built up into cliffs and caves to provide many hideaways for these fish to simulate their natural surroundings in nature; they will need these refuges because they are very possessive about their individual swimming space. If you're smitten with the brilliant colours of these fish, can't necessarily grow aquatic plants but live in a hard water area, then this is the aquarium set up that will satisfy many of your ambitions.

Consider water-flow around the aquarium. Poor water circulation can lead to 'dead spots' where oxygen levels can fall and waste materials collect. Building up an impressive rocky underwater scene may be visually dramatic but uneaten food, dead fish and other debris can build up unseen behind the rockwork to cause water pollution problems.

It is an old trick to use the rockwork to hide the aquarium hardware but again water circulation is important to allow evenness of heating and to avoid blocking the delivery of 'dirty' water to the inlet of the filtration system.

Always make sure that water can circulate freely around the tank, especially in tropical marine aquariums where you may have large colonies of living corals and invertebrates on the rocks which need to have their food delivered to them by the water circulation.

Substrate

The base of the aquarium is generally covered with some type of gravel not just for appearance's sake but to act as a medium in which the aquatic plants can be anchored. Additionally, if a biological filtration system is used then the substrate fulfils the important role of a home for the beneficial nitrifying bacteria to colonize.

Again, care should be taken to choose safe materials for the same reasons previously outlined for rockwork. Particle size should not be too coarse – it will allow uneaten food to drop into it and cause tank pollution – and not too fine otherwise plants will have difficulty in rooting.

The use of coloured gravel is down to personal taste but you must ensure that any colouration does not leach out to discolour the aquarium water.

The marine aquarium confronts the fishkeeper with a slight dilemma: should a substrate be used or not? One argument says that a deep substrate is asking for trouble, whilst opponents say that some fish like to burrow in it, especially at night, and their needs should be considered. It is usually possible to find a compromise somewhere. Deep substrates are no longer normally required since filtration methods have developed beyond the rather outdated undergravel, biological systems that were mandatory in earlier times.

09

the desirable residence

In this chapter you will learn:
- the best place to put the aquarium
- how to set up the aquarium
- getting the aquarium ready for fish.

Before you start to install your aquarium, be sure that you have everything to hand, all the component parts, the right tools, a good working plan plus enough time to do it without having to abandon things part way through.

Tank siting and preparation

The first task is to select the best site for the tank. The idea of brightening up that dark alcove is probably a good idea but make sure a comfortable viewing position is possible near to the tank – an armchair is the ideal aquarium accessory. Having to stand, or crouch down, when viewing the aquarium is not satisfactory for any length of time – and you'll be spending plenty of hours by the tank without a doubt.

Siting the tank near doorways or radiators is not a good idea as either the vibration from the opening and closing of the door, cold draughts entering the room on one hand and extra heat from the radiator on the other will not make for stable water temperatures. Having an aquarium near to 'passing traffic' might well acclimatize the fish to having people constantly moving near to the tank, but the risk is also there of accidental collisions.

The weight of the finished fully-furnished aquarium also has to be considered. Adding up the weight of water (1 kg per litre, 10 lb per gallon) alone is a little daunting but, with the addition of substrate, rockwork and the weight of the tank itself, the final weight can be very high.

In order to support this weight, the aquarium must be sited on a firm surface which, in turn must be adequately supported by the floor. Try to arrange the aquarium's supporting stand or cabinet so that the weight is distributed across the floor joists. Bureaux or sideboards are not recommended pieces of furniture on which to stand an aquarium. Most aquarium manufacturers have associated stands to accompany specific models of aquariums in their catalogues; these are generally of a 'flat pack' nature requiring just a few minutes' work with a screwdriver to assemble.

Apart from avoiding the 'pet shop' look in your lounge, aquarium cabinet stands can effectively hide filtration equipment, wiring, foods, nets, etc. in built-in cupboards below the aquarium itself.

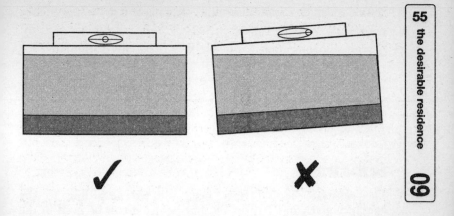

figure 14 it is essential that the tank is level

One very important point is that the aquarium must also be perfectly level, both back to front as well as from side to side; this is not just so the water level looks parallel to the top of the aquarium frame but to avoid unequal pressures being built up on the glass panels which may otherwise crack.

When standing the aquarium on its selected support, a slab of reasonable thickness polystyrene placed under the tank will cushion the tank and also absorb any unevenness between the tank and the supporting base which, again, might put a strain on the bottom glass panel.

If the aquarium is to be sited in an alcove, don't forget to put any background on to the tank before putting it into its final position – it's a little late once the tank's filled up! Similarly, ensure there is reasonable access to the tank and any associated power sockets nearby. It is recommended that a residual current device (RCD) or a residual current circuit breaker (RCCB) is used to protect against electrical shock should a short-circuit occur with any of the aquarium equipment.

It may be prudent to test the tank for leaks before actually putting it in place. It's best to do this outside (just in case) and away from carpets. Place the tank on a firm, level surface and fill with water. Let the tank stand for a few minutes. Closely inspect all joints for 'weeping' and remember that whilst water may collect at the bottom, the actual leak may be higher up.

Should a leak be found then empty the tank and dry it thoroughly.

- Working in a well-ventilated area, seal the inside of the tank with silicon sealant (only use those specially formulated for aquarium use as kitchen/bathroom sealants aren't suitable).
- Run a thin continuous bead of sealant along all inside joints, smoothing it into each joint with a wet finger.
- Leave the tank to 'cure' for at least 24 hours, after which time the tank can be used.

Substrate

The substrate should have been selected according to the guidance given in Chapter 08, but before it can be used in the aquarium it should be washed to remove any excess dust. This is a straightforward procedure if undertaken in easy stages. The amount of substrate required may be considerable if the tank is large and some 'aquascaping' is planned with areas of deep substrate. It is advisable to only wash, say, half a bucket of material at a time: firstly, it's easier to clean this amount and secondly, even half a bucket of wet substrate is enough to carry at once!

Simply half fill a bucket with substrate and, running water continuously into the material, just keep turning the substrate over with your hands or a suitable trowel until the water overflowing from the bucket runs clear. Needless to say, this process is best done outdoors. As each measure is cleaned it can be emptied into the waiting tank, which should by now be in its final position.

However, should you intend to use biological filtration (or even a sub-gravel heating system), then the necessary filter plate (or heating cable) has to be put into the empty tank ahead of the substrate material.

To protect your final aquascaping effects being ruined by digging fish (and the filter plate being exposed), you can lay a piece of plastic mesh material (the area of the aquarium base) on top of the first 2 cms (1") or so of substrate material before putting the final layers on top.

You can slope the contours of the gravel back up from the front of the tank to give a more appealing view, although this tends to flatten out with time. Construct terraces, to provide dramatic planting pockets, by pushing pieces of thin slate into the substrate at an angle to hold back the deeper layers of substrate.

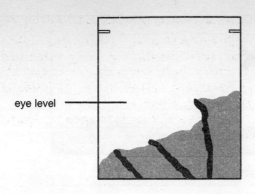

eye level

figure 15 making terraces

Substrate in marine aquariums

With undergravel (biological) filtration now outmoded by the use of living rock and protein skimmers, there is a growing preference to have a minimal covering of substrate material in the marine aquarium; some argue that having none at all is even better. But we come to the requirement of some fishes, such as the Yellow-faced Jawfish, and invertebrates such as Pistol Shrimps that like to burrow in the gravel to make homes, or fish such as some Wrasses that like to burrow into the substrate each night.

A practicable solution to this is to have just a separate area of the tank floor with a deep layer of substrate; some achieve this by using a shallow plastic container (a miniature seed tray, for example) filled with substrate.

The problem found in freshwater aquariums with using calcareous materials does not arise in the marine aquarium. Generally a combination of crushed coral sand and small pieces of broken coral give the correct look to the marine aquarium if you want to have a substrate.

Hardware

As electricity and water make extremely bad companions, it pays to play safe at all times when installing equipment. A good rule is never to switch on any submersible aquarium equipment unless it is under water.

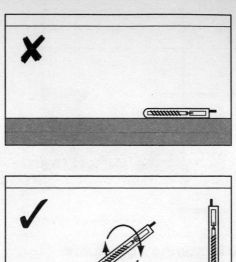

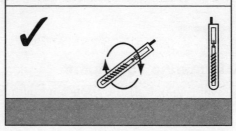

figure 16a the wrong position for a heater

figure 16b the correct position(s) for a heater

Rather than have a jumble of cables to various pieces of aquarium equipment, the use of a 'cable tidy' is highly recommended. This neat box, which fixes to the side of the tank, is a miniature switching and power distribution centre. Supplies for equipment that works 24 hours a day, such as heaters, are not switched but those for lighting and pumps are.

The first, and most important, rule is: **never take a heater out of water until it has cooled down**. Also, never test a heater out of water; it will heat up very quickly and you'll probably drop it and also burn yourself too.

Mount a heater in the tank, so that it has enough water circulating flow around it; don't lay it on the substrate.

If you have a large tank, then split the tank's heating requirements between two thermostat/heater units: this helps spread the heat evenly and faster through the tank and you've got a 'back-up' heater should one of the pair fail.

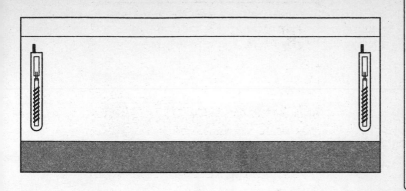

figure 17 two heaters spread heat more evenly in large tanks

Once the heaters are in place, connect them to the non-switchable terminals in the cable tidy, but **do not switch the unit on.**

Filters

Filters should be positioned in the tank so that the returning water is directed away from the filter's immediate vicinity so that a water circulation pattern is established around the aquarium. This is easily achieved by turning the return spout on the filter or, in the case of external filters, the inlet and outlet connecting hoses can be at opposite ends of the tank.

Some large external filters are equipped with a spraybar return that distributes the returning water over the surface of the water rather than through a single spout. This creates less disturbance in the tank.

For ease of maintenance, it's a good idea to fit isolating taps in each of the connecting hoses to an external filter. These allow you to switch off the water-flow to, and from, the filter so that it can be removed for cleaning without the need for re-priming when re-connected again.

Again, power cables for the filters can be connected to the relevant connectors in the cable tidy. Only switch on filters when internal types are fully submerged or external ones fully primed with water.

If an undergravel (biological) filter is used, fit the airstone into the uplift tube and connect it to the air-pump via a length of neoprene air-line making sure there is either an 'anti-siphon' loop made in its path or a non-return valve fitted.

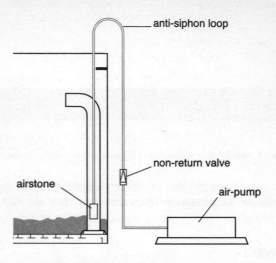

figure 18 protection against water damage to the pump

Either of these precautions will ensure water is not sucked back into the pump should a power cut occur. Failing that, site the pump above the tank.

Marine aquariums are fitted with protein skimmers. These may vary in design and be used both inside or outside the tank.

Outside models may necessitate the hood being cut to accommodate the units, whilst the dimensions of internal skimmers must be checked so that they fit not only inside the tank but also under the hood. Again, electrically powered models can be connected to the cable tidy but not switched on until the tank is full of water. Air-operated types must be connected to the air-pump and you must prevent back-siphoning as discussed above for undergravel filters.

Although fitted, don't expect the protein skimmer to do its job immediately. It will take a little time for the organic material to build up in the tank and this won't happen until livestock have been introduced.

Decoration

To ensure that wood does not float when placed in the tank, stick it to a flat piece of slate – using silicone sealant, or use a plastic, non-metallic screw – and then bury the slate in the substrate. The weight of the substrate will keep the wood down.

You need to make sure that any rock formation you create is stable and not liable to topple over and break the aquarium glass.

It is possible to create rocky outcrops by gluing together several pieces of rock with silicone sealant prior to placing them in the aquarium. Make sure they are embedded in the substrate rather than just being placed on its surface. Another way to stabilize rocks, especially in large deep tanks is to suspend them by thin nylon filaments (or out-of-sight cable wraps) from a cross-member on the top of the tank.

Do not obstruct water-flow around the tank when hiding 'hardware' especially to heaters and filter inlets.

If you are creating a marine aquarium and intend using 'living rock,' you must not place the rock in the 'dry' aquarium but wait until the tank has been filled with water and the correct amount of salt mix added. It may be worth postponing buying 'living rock' until after the aquarium set up has reached this stage. There is no problem with installing a base foundation of decorative rocks or pieces of dead coral at this time.

Water

Once the aquascaping has been finished and the hardware installed, it is time to fill the aquarium. Before the water can be added, it should be treated either, in the case of tap water, with a dechlorinator to neutralize the chlorine or, for marine aquariums, synthetic sea water must be prepared. In the case of *the intial setting up* of the marine aquarium the salt mix can be made up in the newly-filled tank but, subsequently, for partial water changes, the new sea water must be mixed in buckets separately from the main tank.

The quality of the water used to mix the synthetic sea water must not be overlooked. Nitrate and phosphate are often found in tap water and as these are known 'nutrients' of troublesome algae it would be best if water used for mixing did not contain such minerals.

Tap water can be treated ahead of use to remove nitrate and phosphate, although many marine fishkeepers prefer to use water treated by reverse osmosis filters. RO water, as it is known, can be obtained in large quantities from your aquatic dealer.

To avoid all your hard aquascaping work being 'flattened' by the incoming water, place a shallow saucer or even a shallow jug on the substrate and direct the water into that. The water will then overflow into the tank without causing any further disturbance.

Once the tank has been filled with water, the heating system should be switched on and the water temperature allowed to rise to its pre-defined setting. This is because the specific gravity reading shown by the hydrometer is temperature-sensitive and tests should only be made at the right water temperature if you want a true reading is to be obtained. An airstone should be added to provide some water circulation to assist in the dissolving process and also vent off excess carbon dioxide.

Just under the approximate amount of synthetic salt mix should be added to the aquarium and the tank left for an hour or so to let the salt fully dissolve before testing the SG.

• Test the SG of the water with the hydrometer. As you have 'under-dosed' you will probably need to add more salt but only add small amounts at a time.
• Continue this process and testing until the correct SG is reached.
• Should you have added too much salt right from the start, resulting in a too high a SG, then you must take out some tank water and replace it with fresh (not salty) water.
• Let the tank settle for a while and then re-test.
• Adjust, using more salt, or replacing with fresh water until the correct reading is achieved.

If you intend to put plants in the freshwater aquarium, then don't completely fill the aquarium with water. The reason for this will be explained later in this chapter.

Planting

You can, of course, plant the freshwater aquarium as soon as there is substrate in it, but the advantage of planting when it is almost full of water is that the plants instantly take up their natural positions, as opposed to just flopping over on the substrate, and you can then see the immediate result (or not!) of your aquascaping skills. The reason for not filling the tank completely before planting, if you haven't already guessed, is simple – you put your arms in the tank to plant, and displaced water spills out of the tank!

It is debatable whether you should switch on the heater to warm up the water before planting but, it has to be said, it's a lot more comfortable working in warm water than plunging your hands into cold water.

Just like fish, plants look better in groups: plant six or so plants of the same species in a clump for a more realistic look. When planting, do not bury the junction between any 'stem' and the root system otherwise the plant may rot away quite quickly. Avoid damaging any roots when putting them into the substrate.

Plants may come from the supplier in different presentations. Often, rooted plants are offered for sale in miniature plastic pots with the plant's roots contained in a nutrient rich rockwool wrapping. Others, typically those that are offered as 'cuttings' may be just bundled together with a thin strip of lead around the stems.

There is a divided opinion about what to do with those potted specimens with respect to the rockwool. Some advocate burying everything and letting the plant use up the nutrients whilst others say that the rockwool eventually gets dislodged by foraging fish and bits of it continually float around the aquarium. It is not difficult to unwrap the rockwool, just unroll it, and root the plant in the substrate as normal.

With the lead-wrapped specimens, discard the lead strip from those plants which have established roots and again plant normally; lead-weighted 'cutting' can be left in the tank until new rootlets have formed on the plant stems and then the cutting can be re-rooted as usual.

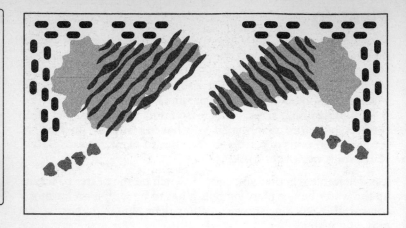

figure 19 a suggested planting plan: top view

This planting plan shows how to hide the back and sides of the tank (tall grass-type plants are ideal for this) whilst more bushy species fill out other spaces. Low foreground plants help add an illusion of 'front-to-back' depth in the tank. Details of typical species of plants to use may be found in Chapter 07.

Try to offset the planting plan so that the tank has a more natural look rather than a symmetrical design. Avoid centrally-placed specimen plants too. A plain background colour to the back of the aquarium also helps to add a receding 'distance' effect.

With one or two pieces of bogwood or rockwork, the glass box effect has been disguised.

Apart from growths of algae which is some cases can be permitted for the benefit of herbivorous fishes, the only living 'green' decoration you could introduce into the marine aquarium would be macro-algae mainly of the genus *Caulerpa*. This family of 'mini-seaweeds' seems to have a dual personality – it grows splendidly but then may suddenly die off and fill the aquarium with bright green water. If you are prepared to take the risk or find the trick of restricting its suicidal tendencies then *Caulerpa* does add that missing 'plant' dimension to the marine aquarium.

figure 20 the addition of bogwood/rockwool to an aquarium: front view

Marine corals

Once the marine aquarium water is up to correct temperature and of the correct SG it will be safe to introduce the 'living rock' and a few soft corals.

Unlike plants, corals cannot be 'planted' in clumps. Many have stinging cells and/or are intolerant of close neighbours. You should leave adequate gaps between corals to allow for this and for the fact that they will grow.

Not all corals require the same lighting levels. As with plants, it is better to site the low light-loving species in the relative shade, beneath an overhanging rock for instance.

You can always move species up into brighter conditions at a later date if necessary; always move the coral complete on its rock rather than prising it off and hoping it will relocate successfully.

You may have a location problem when dealing with Sea Anemones: they have a mind of their own and will move around the aquarium to find their own favourite spot, usually just where you don't want them – on the front glass or over a filter inlet!

It is also recommended that you introduce a 'cleaner gang' – a few Hermit Crabs and Snails – that will take care of any algae that might develop during the tank's maturation period, as the aquarium awaits the arrival of the fish.

Finishing off

When the tank has been planted and all the other decorations put in place, you can then fill the tank to the appropriate level.

Place the cover glass in position on the 'shelves.' Whilst plastic one-piece 'condensation trays' are available (or may come supplied with the tank), making your own cover glass can make a practical difference. Having the cover glass in two pieces means that either part can be slid to one side for access to the tank and to feed the fish.

Place the hood in position and connect the lighting cable to a switched terminal on the cable tidy. The air-pump, fitted with airline and a non-return valve, can also be similarly connected.

Internal filters will be primed automatically by the rising water in the tank, but external filters must be primed. Many modern external filters have automatic priming devices but here's how to do it manually:

• Open both isolation taps fully.
• Disconnect the outlet hose from the spraybar, or just unhook the return hose from where it enters the tank, and suck briefly on the open hose. Water will be drawn down the inlet hose and into the filter and rise back up the outlet hose.
• Hold the end of the outlet hose higher than the aquarium until you see the water level reach the same level as that in the tank.
• Reconnect the outlet hose or hook it back into the tank.

Now the filter can be switched on:

• Check for leaks at all hose and isolating tap connectors.
• Check that water is following out of the spraybar or return tube into the tank, and not on to the carpet!

Operate the aquarium lights as though fish were present. This will assist the plants to become established ahead of any possible disturbing effects, such as the arrival of the fish.

Maturation

Sad to say, after all the hard work of learning about what to do, and doing it, there's still a somewhat lengthy period to wait before you can safely introduce fish into your newly-set-up

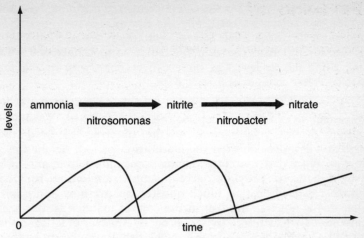

figure 21 the maturation process in newly-set-up aquarium or newly-installed filtration system

aquarium. The problem is that the tank needs to biologically settle down, or 'mature.' It's the ammonia, nitrite, nitrate story all over again but it's just a matter of time before you start living the aquarist's dream.

Testing the water

How do you know when it's safe to introduce fish? There are three distinct development stages, and you can test the progress of the tank's maturation at each stage using the appropriate ammonia, nitrite and nitrate test kits.

Simply put the right amount of water to be tested in the phial supplied in the test kit; add the reagent as directed (you may have to add two in some cases) and watch the colour change accordingly. Compare this colour against the supplied colour reference chart and read off the value of whatever element you are testing for.

If you test the water in a newly set up aquarium from day 1, you will find that the ammonia levels slowly rise to a peak and then drop rapidly. After a few days, nitrite levels mirror the same rise and fall as the ammonia levels after which time nitrates make an appearance and gradually mount up.

These occurrences reflect the establishment of nitrifying bacteria within the aquarium, especially the filtration system, and it is not until the nitrite levels fall to a minimum that the aquarium is safe for fish to be introduced. Don't be too concerned with any rising nitrate levels as these can be dealt with by regular partial water changes at a later date.

Is there any way this process can be accelerated? To those impatient would-be fishkeepers, the answer is 'yes.' Adding a culture of nitrifying bacteria to the aquarium to 'seed' the system will indeed shorten the maturation period. At one time, it was advocated that introducing some 'nitrite-tolerant' fish would help to provide decomposing ammunition for the bacteria to feed on that much quicker, but we now appreciate that this is not treating fish in the correct manner as they will undoubtedly be stressed by this process. Another practical tip is to add a small amount of food to the fishless aquarium so that as it decomposes this too helps to mature the tank.

The consequences of introducing fish too early, never mind too many, would be to encourage an explosion of nitrite and suffer what's become known as New Tank Syndrome – in other words, a wipe-out.

But there's a bright side to all this foreboding. You can certainly watch your tank as it matures, seeing the plants become established and, in the marine tank, the development of invertebrate life emerging from the living rock. At the same time, you should use this waiting period to thoroughly research the fish you are going to introduce, so that you can give them all the desirable residence they undoubtedly deserve.

10

friends and neighbours

In this chapter you will learn:
- how to buy suitable fish
- how fish names are classified
- about the various groups of popular fishes.

Buying fish

At this time, you can probably imagine yourself at the aquatic store faced with selecting your fish, but what will you choose? Even with the narrowest area of interest, coldwater fishkeeping, there is still a wide variety of fishes to look at and evaluate. But before you hand over the cash, you ought to know some more about choosing fish rather than just hoping for the best.

The basic rules of buying fish are:

• Always buy healthy stock.
• Buy compatible stock.
• Know the adult size the fish will attain.
• Don't buy too many at once.
• Be guided by the dealer.
• Buy responsibly.

It's important to buy healthy stock simply because you don't want your new fish to be short-lived for one thing and, in future times, neither do you want it to introduce disease into the tank to infect fish you may already have.

Sadly, not all fish make good aquarium tenants in the context of keeping them in a community collection. Obviously if you can provide the right conditions for any fish you can keep it in a tank either on its own or as part of a single-species collection.

In the natural world it is an inescapable fact that big things eat little things so you shouldn't let this state of affairs arise in the aquarium. You should realize that all fish offered for sale are likely to be juveniles – it makes for better transportation costs (and profits) if you can get more fish in the bag.

The snag arises when not all these juvenile fish grow at the same rate once in your aquarium. Those appealing looking Oscars, with their marbled markings will eventually turn out to be ugly great brutes (my personal opinion!) around the 25 cm mark whilst the pretty Tetras you bought with them haven't grown much more than another centimetre. It may be that the Oscars won't actually eat the smaller fish but just being in the same tank can cause the smaller fishes some distress as their larger tank mates swim by. Try to get some idea of the growth rate of your fish and their eventual size, before you buy.

It's not only differences in size that makes for incompatible tank mates. Not all fish need the same water conditions and it may prove a fruitless exercise to keep, say, hard water-loving fish with those that are much happier in soft water.

You will find, in the marine aquarium, some fish simply cannot abide other fish having the same colour as themselves, and this attitude may even extend to members of their own genus; one does wonder sometimes how these species ever manage to breed!

Many fish, especially the smaller, decorative species look a lot better when kept in a shoal. Fish usually find security in numbers (a natural defence against predators) so why not pander to them? There's no need to buy dozens, maybe six or eight will provide the comfort they seek and the visual sight you desire. Again, it's finding out in advance which species are naturally gregarious and which are the loners that will make or break your aquarium's attractiveness.

There is also the tendency among newcomers to the hobby to be tempted to buy too many on their first fish-buying expedition. The result, apart from financial damage to the credit card, is that the tank is hopelessly overcrowded, the filtration is unable to cope and a massive ammonia build-up occurs and the whole tank is wiped out. Hardly the start you wished for.

Once you get settled in the hobby, the chances are that you will become a regular customer at the aquatic store. By cultivating a relationship with the dealer your aquarium will benefit; the dealer will know what you've bought in the past, can advise as to what would make good compatible (that word again) companions and also be in the best place to let you know of any future developments in the shop – new equipment or new fishes coming in, etc. The very best dealers actually refuse to sell fish if they suspect that their destined home is either not prepared for them or that they know that some newly-imported fish aren't quite ready to come out of the quarantine section just yet.

By patronizing your local aquatic store, you stand a better chance of keeping the fish successfully than if you buy fish at a more distant store. This is because your local dealer is more likely to be keeping his fish in the same water conditions that are available to you.

Buying fish is not just a matter of marching into the aquatic store, handing over the cash and taking home what you fancy. Responsibility should play a big part in the process. Don't be tempted to buy fish you won't be able to look after; this is particularly relevant in marine fishkeeping where some of the most desirable, albeit expensive, species have very specialized dietary needs which often prove impossible to meet, with the result that the fish simply starves to death over a period of time.

Another area where fishkeepers might wish to exercise some kind of control is by not buying fish that have been injected with colour dyes, been bred using genetically-modified materials or, should you feel strongly enough, man-made variations featuring distended bodies, extra-long finnage, etc. of popular species.

Populating the tank

As we have already discovered, the position of the mouth tells you all about where the fish swims in the water. You can use this knowledge to select suitably appropriate fishes, swimming at the top, middle and bottom levels in the tank, and make sure your aquarium has its full complement of fishes, from top to bottom. You will find details helpful notes on this aspect in the following section.

Quick guide to fish groups

It would be an impossible task to list all fish together in a massive A–Z ranking. We take advantage of taxonomic classification to divide fishes into small groups, ranging down through phylum, class, super-order, order, family, etc. Fishkeepers are only concerned with the bottom rungs of this ladder, at family level and below.

Once at family level, the main identifying labels are the genus name, analogous to our surname, and the specific name, corresponding to our forename. In writing, the generic name is always capitalized, the specific name lower case.

This binomial system of naming animals, created by Carl von Linné (Linnaeus), gives each animal a distinct two-part name. Different animals can have the same specific name – 'reticulatus' for instance means 'netting-like pattern' – so you have *Corydoras reticulatus* (a Catfish), *Hyphessobrycon reticulatus* (a Tetra) as well as *Python reticulatus* (a Snake) and *Dendrobates reticulatus* (a Tree Frog) but no two different animals can share the same genus, or generic, name.

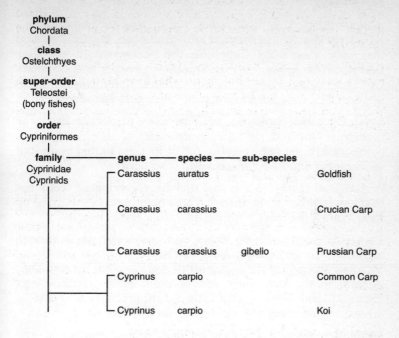

figure 22 the classification of fish

For the purposes of fishkeeping, a number of group names have been used, and it usually turns out to be an accepted mixture of common names and scientific names.

Tropical fishes

Typical tropical fish groups are: Cyprinids, Characins, Cichlids, Labyrinthfish, Killifish, Catfish, Loaches, Rainbowfish and livebearers.

Within these headings, sub-divisions also occur. For instance, the very large Cyprinid group contains not only tropical Barbs, Rasboras and Danios but also coldwater fish such as Goldfish and Koi too. Livebearers include Guppies, Swordtails, Platys and Mollies.

Cyprinids

(Colour Plates 3, 4, 5, 6) Fishes in the Cyprinid family form a very large part of the interest of fishkeeping. It might be said that, if it wasn't for Cyprinids, the hobby would not have flourished for it was a very humble Cyprinid, the Common Goldfish (Colour Plate 2), that set the hobby on it way hundreds of years ago, long before 'tropicals' were first introduced.

Most Cyprinids look like most people's idea of a fish. The mouth is located on the centre-line of the body and, consequently, the fish spends most of its time in mid-water but visits higher and lower levels when it so desires.

A feature of these fishes is that they have specialized teeth, not in the mouth but in the throat. These pharyngeal teeth grind up food against the fish's hard palate, rather than chew it.

Cyprinids are egg-laying fishes and most use the scattering method when spawning (the Harlequin Rasbora bucks the trend by laying its eggs on the underside of aquatic plant leaves). They are not in the least interested in their newly-fertilized eggs except as food. When breeding these fish, precaution have to be taken to prevent eggs being lost in this way (see Chapter 15).

Popular tropical Cyprinids include Barbs, Rasboras, and Danios. These are, in the main, modest-sized and make colourful subjects. Whilst Barbs and Rasboras tend to use most of the water depth, the more lively Danios normally choose the upper levels where they add constant activity to the scene, especially if they are kept in a shoal.

Keeping Cyprinids presents no problems as they are hardy fishes, with hearty appetites to match, accepting almost anything in the way of food. Many are easily bred in captivity and members of the Danio genus are often recommended species for anyone wishing to try their hand at breeding for the first time.

Originating mostly in Asia and India, they are widely available at all aquatic outlets.

Characins

(Colour Plates 7, 8, 9, 10) Characins might be regarded as the South American counterpart of the Cyprinids although a large number also come from Africa.

This group also contains a huge number of aquarium-suitable species. All members of the Characin group have sharp teeth in the jaws, regardless of size; at one end of the scale, you have the brilliantly-coloured diminutive Neon Tetra whilst at the other extreme is the considerably larger Piranha!

In between these two, there are lots of highly-decorative fish to bring colour to the aquarium. Male Characins often have extended finnage and both sexes have that 'extra' fin, the adipose, situated on the back in between the main dorsal fin and the tail. A typical Tetra will have a symmetrically shaped body, a deep belly and a highly-arched back. Naturally, these fish occupy the mid-water level.

Characins provide long-standing favourites for the aquarium and are equally easy to keep. Some of the larger species have an appetite for aquarium plants.

Genera to look out for particularly are *Hyphessobrycon* and *Hemigrammus* both of which offer many brilliantly coloured, modest-sized species. These are usually described as Tetras. Closely-related, but cylindrically-bodied, are the Pencilfishes of the genus *Nannostomus* which can make an ideal subject for a small 'one-species' aquarium.

Characins are also egg-scattering fishes and the breeding method description given earlier for Cyprinids applies equally here, although one exception is the Splashing Tetra, *Copella arnoldi*, which actually lays its eggs out of water (on an overhanging plant leaf, in case you're wondering) away from its natural predators.

Cichlids

(Colour Plates 11, 12, 13, 14) Now this is where it gets really interesting. To many fishkeepers, Cichlids are ugly brutes who think nothing of re-arranging the aquarium's decorations when it suits them although, to be fair to the fish, they usually do it when breeding and, understandably, are only staking out their breeding territory.

Cichlids come in diverse shapes, sizes and colours originating in Central and South America, Africa and Asia. Central American species are generally the tough guys; South America offers the highly-coloured *Apistogramma* genus, the stately Discus (Colour Plate 12) and everyone's favourite, the Angelfish (Colour Plate 11). Not to be outdone, Africa holds its own with the dazzling colours of its Rift Valley fishes (Colour Plate 14), many of which are endemic to each particular lake. For a region so normally blessed with fishes, Asia is a poor third with only two or three Cichlids native to its waters.

So there's an ample choice to attract you, but the real attraction for most fishkeepers is that these fish are parents par excellence. All cichlids are egg-depositors, females laying their eggs on a firm surface for the male to fertilize, but there are variations on this basic premise. The majority are happy to prepare a spawning site in open water, then fertilize and defend their hatching eggs against all-comers. For the fishkeeper, this makes a very watchable process.

Taking parental care a little further, some species get very secretive about their breeding and prefer to do it in the privacy of a rocky cave, a flowerpot or even a vacant large shell, well away from their owner's prying eyes.

Others, some African Lake species, only just make it into the egg-depositing category; in these cases, the female does lay eggs (usually in a depression in the substrate) but then as the male fertilizes them she picks up the eggs and incubates them in her throat cavity until the young fish are developed enough to swim free. Even then, her task is not over for, at the slightest threat, the fry all dash back into her mouth for safety.

Another feature of Cichlids, is that the fry of Discus is noted for finding its first food in the mucus covering of its parents' skin. When one parent has had enough of being a feeding station the fry are flicked towards the other to continue their meal.

Caring for Cichlids is both straightforward and complicated, depending on which species you choose. Central American and African Lake species are hard water loving, whilst South American fish are better suited to soft water; Discus require more stringent water management than most.

Feeding is no problem as most are omnivorous although some African Lake species will need green matter in their diet as they normally graze on algae-covered rocks in their natural home.

As you can appreciate, tenancy of territory plays a strong role in these fishes' life style, so any aquarium destined for Cichlid inhabitants (and they occupy all levels) must be large enough to give each fish their allotted space – or there will be constant skirmishes between rival house-hunters.

Labyrinthfish

(Colour Plates 19, 20, 21, 22) For a quieter aquarium try members of this group. Gouramies are gentle creatures as, armed with their constantly 'enquiring' outstretched pelvic fins, they explore every corner of the tank.

Although these Asia-based fish are physically equipped to survive under deteriorating water conditions in their jungle pools and creeks thanks to their auxiliary breathing organ, they should not be subjected to these conditions in captivity.

Most will use a bubble-nest during spawning. The male fish constructs a floating nest of bubbles using saliva to bind the bubbles and attracts the female beneath it, where he embraces her, flips her on her back so that the expelled, and immediately fertilized, eggs float up into the nest. Any that fall downwards, he will pick up and return them to the nest where they will hatch under his constant guard.

That's the theory. Sometimes, if the male considers the female not ready to spawn he will attack her, so the spawning is best supervised, or at least the aquarium should have plenty of plants in which the rejected female can hide. Even in the event of a happy outcome, the female should be removed after spawning is complete.

The Siamese Fighting Fish (Colour Plate 21) is a special case. Although it can be kept in the normal community aquarium, only one male at a time can be kept as otherwise fierce battles ensue with death as the likely outcome for the loser. There are many aquarium-created colour varieties of this species, *Betta splendens*, but these modern day species with their exaggerated finnage are far removed from the natural fish.

Sizes of Gouramies range from modest to enormous (some are considered excellent food fish in their native countries); most are peaceful, hardy community fish although some males can wreak havoc when defending their bubble-nest. Generally they use the middle and upper levels of the aquarium.

Although many can be bred, the fry are often smaller than expected and care should be taken to have enough of the correct (microscopic) sized food ready if the fry are to make it to adulthood. As these fish are air-breathers to some extent, some fishkeepers advise keeping the tank covered during the fry-rearing period so that any draughts are prevented from entering the hood lest the fry breathe in the cold air which could prove fatal.

Killifish

(Colour Plates 23, 24) Yet again, a family of fish with a difference. Killifish (the word 'killi' means 'ditch') are small brilliantly-coloured cylindrical fish inhabiting the upper layers of the water. Found in South America and in Africa, they are short-lived which has led to them also being known as 'annual fishes' although many extend their lives in the aquarium beyond the theoretical 12 month cut-off point.

It is difficult to categorize their breeding pattern as it varies according to species. Some lay eggs in plants, or special 'spawning mops' made by their owner (see Chapter 15) but others have developed an incredible method to ensure survival of the species. This is vitally important when you consider that the water in which they live may dry up each season.

Burying the fertilized eggs in the riverbed mud is the answer, but the real brilliance of the idea is yet to come. The eggs are 'programmed' to begin hatching once the rainy season comes; apart from releasing the eggs from the mud, the torrential rains also wash extra food – insects, etc. – into the water ready to feed the emerging young fish. But suppose the first rainfall is just a shower and doesn't refill the streambed?

Only a small proportion of the eggs hatch at the first rainfall. A second dousing is usually required for the main batch to hatch.

Breeding Killifish entails simulating Nature to a degree. The fishes' eggs can be gathered from where they are laid and stored for a period of time in a semi-dry condition. Re-immersing them should trigger hatching but, as in the natural world, a second immersion may be needed to ensure the whole batch hatches out.

The facility of the eggs to withstand semi-dehydration means that they can be easily transported. Many Killifish owners take advantage of this to exchange eggs by post (even inter-continentally) to build up stocks of the fish in captivity.

Because of their size, Killifish do not need a large aquarium, a 25-litre tank is their idea of a wide open space. Some water management beyond the normal may be necessary and many Killifish tanks have a brownish tinge to the water where peat has been used to acidify it. Again, because of their special breeding methods (some actually plough into a deep peat-based substrate), they are best kept in separate species collections.

Catfish

(Colour Plates 29, 30) From one level of the tank to the other extreme. Catfish live on the bottom of the aquarium. It is not correct to treat Catfish as scavengers, depending on them to clear up any food left by the other fish and hoping they will survive on this infrequent diet. They should be cared for like any other fish and their needs satisfied just as assiduously.

All Catfish have taste-bud equipped barbels around their mouths which enables them to locate their food as they forage around on the substrate. There is hardly any curvature to the bottom profile of their bodies and this allows them to get their underslung mouths even closer to the substrate. It is important that the substrate is kept clean as any decomposing matter will harbour bacteria which, in turn, will cause problems to the fish. Some advocate using soft sand as substrate to lessen 'wear and tear' on the fish's barbels.

Not all Catfish have scales; some have just skin and are referred to as 'naked' whilst others are covered with hard overlapping bony plates, 'scutes'. Another feature of some species is the ability to 'lock up' the large dorsal fin; this serves the fish well as it prevents it being swallowed by a predator or being withdrawn from an underwater crevice by fishermen.

A popular genus is the South American *Corydoras* (Colour Plate 30), with around 150 species to choose from. These small gregarious Catfish also have a fascinating breeding procedure. The female fish carries eggs to their selected hatching area by holding them between her pelvic fins. Another characteristic of this genus, together with some other species, is the ability to use atmospheric air, gulped at the surface; oxygen is extracted using part of the hind gut, and the used air is expelled through the fish's vent.

Many Catfish are nocturnal by nature. This fact often hides the fact that some are predatory, especially the very large species such as the Red Tailed Catfish, *Phractocephalus hemioliopterus* which, in truth, should not be considered suitable for the average aquarium as many outgrow their quarters within a very short space of time.

Catfish should be fed with fast-sinking foods so that it escapes the attentions of mid-water fishes on the way down. Additionally, some food should also be given late at night, perhaps after the aquarium lights have been switched off, for the benefit of nocturnal species. One service that some Catfish are only too happy to provide is that of algae-removal. Large Suckermouth Catfish, *Hypostomus* sp., can clear up a green-infested tank in no time but it is then important to maintain vegetable matter in their diet once the algae has been cleared. Lettuce and courgettes are often relished and, should you furnish the aquarium with ornamental bogwood, don't be surprised if some Catfish take to munching on it.

Impressive though some of the larger Catfish may be, some are very predatory, beginning their quest for food as dusk falls and often extending their efforts to satisfy their appetites throughout the night.

Loaches

(Colour Plates 31, 32) Remaining on the aquarium floor, Loaches are also popular species. Whilst their bodies may be flattened on the ventral contour, some have a stocky cylindrical body whilst others resemble miniature Eels. The popular members of the *Botia* genus and the Kuhli Loach, *Pangio* sp., all have erectile spines below the eye: the Kuhli Loach's former taxonomic name, *Acanthophthalmus*, literally translated means 'Prickle-, or Thorn-eye.' This makes netting the fish problematic as the spines get caught in the net very easily – that's if you can get the fish into the net in the first place as they are very adept at not being caught, especially in a well-planted tank!

Most Loaches are nocturnal, preferring to lay up during the daytime amongst the aquatic plants before venturing out after 'lights-out'. Many have a habit of making clicking noises by expelling water forcibly through their gills; other peculiar habits include laying on their side (especially after a meal) or diving into the substrate, a tendency they employ when introduced into a new, unfamiliar aquarium.

Loaches are meat eaters and can be tempted out of their daytime hideaways by feeding worm-foods such as Whiteworm or some other live food. Many Loaches provide the added attraction of being able to rid the aquarium of snails.

The *Botia* genus, from India and the Far East, has very small scales giving the body covering, a skin-like quality; this genus is reported to be susceptible to some proprietary remedies when treating for White Spot for example.

Rainbowfish

(Colour Plates 25, 26, 27, 28) Australia, being a continent in isolation, does not have such a variety of genera as other continents but what it lacks in quantity it makes up for with quality. Rainbowfishes, also from neighbouring New Guinea, are quite unmistakeable, having very pointed snouts, usually with a definite notch immediately above the eye whose appearance is exaggerated by the highly-arched back that comes with increasing age. A feature that also sets the Rainbowfish apart from other fish is the presence of two separate dorsal fins.

Rainbowfish are constantly active, usually in the upper layers of the aquarium; they like hard water and are extremely gregarious. They require a large tank if you are to benefit from seeing them at their best, preferably in a large shoal.

Popular Australasian species are *Melanotaenia* and *Glossolepis* but other Rainbowfishes such as *Telmatherina*, *Iriatherina* and *Bedotia* can be found in Indonesia, Sulawesi, and Madagascar respectively.

Livebearers

(Colour Plates 15, 16, 17, 18) Just as the Angelfish and Siamese Fighting Fish are recognized by most people outside of the hobby, so too is the Guppy, *Poecilia reticulata* (Colour Plate 17).

This little fish is known all over the world, not just for its aquarium popularity but also as a very active deterrent in the fight against the malaria-carrying mosquito whose larval form it positively relishes as a meal. In consequence, it has been 'exported' to many tropical malaria-infested countries worldwide from its original home in Trinidad.

The Guppy, (Millions Fish is another of its common names), comes in many variations, especially in the colours and configuration of its fins, notably the tail. Huge selective breeding programmes over the years have resulted in Guppies being available in almost any colour you'd care to choose. Initially, it was only the male fish that attracted all the attention but now, even females are becoming more colourful.

The Swordtail and Platy, from Central America, are two species within the *Xiphophorus* genus but there is no confusing them thanks to the very obvious sword-like extension to the lower part of the tail of the former species, *X. helleri*. The Platy, *X. maculatus*, is a stockier fish but both have been selectively bred into the same man-made colour varieties available today – Hi-Fins, Tuxedo, Wagtail, Simpson, Red-eye Reds, and Marigold are all typical descriptions. Another popular strain is the Variatus Platy, *X. variatus* (Colour Plate 18), which is a 'stretched' version of which the Sunset is a typical example.

The Swordtail (Colour Plate 15) has an interesting characteristic in that it can change sex. It is usually female Swordtails that take on male characteristics. This is not quite so dramatic as sex changes that occur in some marine fishes where, for instance should the dominant male fish die, a female from his harem will change sex to take his place as a fully functional male.

As might be expected, hybridization can take place between species within a genus and this has been used to produce many different strains for the market. It also reinforces the precaution that care must be taken to keep different strains apart when attempting to maintain a pure strain of fishes.

If you need a fish that makes a colourful contrast against the aquatic plants why not go for a jet black species? The velvety Black Molly, *Poecilia sphenops*, fits the requirement ideally. Although silvery-green in nature, Mollies have also been aquarium-bred into other colours and it is quite common to see gold varieties, mostly the *P. latipinna* or *P. velifera* species which have the added attraction of a huge, sail-like dorsal fin too (Colour Plate 16). The Liberty Molly, *P. salvatoris*, is a slender silvery-grey fish with a brilliant red dorsal fin.

There is one species, *P. formosa*, that only exists as females. In order to maintain the species, it must mate with a different Molly species.

Why are they called Mollies? Due to changes in taxonomic classification the original name is no longer used and so the explanation is not so well known; the fish were first described as *Mollienisia* in honour of the French explorer Mollien.

Most the species mentioned have upturned mouths, indicating that they naturally take food from the surface, mainly insect life in nature. Under aquarium conditions, all are hardy and will eat a wide variety of foods. Some are particularly fond of soft algae and will relish some vegetable matter in their diet.

Other livebearers

In addition to the popular cultivated livebearers described above, there are many other 'wild' genera that are becoming increasingly popular. Species include *Limia*, *Gambusia*, *Ameca*, *Xenotoca*, *Dermogenys* and *Brachyrhaphis* and are recommended to be kept in separate 'species' collections rather than in community tanks.

These fishes may not be quite so colourful (although their supporters may deny this) and you may have to seek them out through specialist aquatic groups, as they are not so easily available through the usual aquatic outlets.

Coldwater fishes

Goldfish

(Colour Plate 2) The Common Goldfish must the most commonly-kept fish in the world, althoug its popularity as an aquarium fish has diminished against the hugely popular tropical fishes which are now available, both for freshwater and marine aquariums. Having said that, the Goldfish can still be as source of enjoyment as long a it is treated respectfully, and given a large enough aquarium.

There are several extensions to the Goldfish theme for, although only consisting of one variety, *Carassius auratus*, many years of aquarium breeding have produced several different strains. The London and Bristol Shubunkins are the two most basic 'improvements'. The London has a shorter tail against the Bristol's well-developed broad-lobed tail but it is in the colour development where the attraction lies. Pigmentation under the skin produces violets, blues and reds which, coupled with the non-reflectivity of the scales produce a wide range of colourations quite distinct from the single red/orange colour of the metallic-scaled Common Goldfish.

The Comet, another metallic fish, has a large forked tail almost as long as the body. This specie can swim at high speed but only for short periods.

All of the previously described varieties are suitable for both aquarium and pond culture. They are known as 'singletails' as the tail fin comprises a single unit. The following varieties have double tails and are known as 'twin-tails'.

From here on, the traditional Goldfish body shape has undergone further development and has become more and more egg-shaped. By further selective breeding, more flowing fins have been added, in some cases the dorsal fin lost, eyes have become telescopic and tails flattened and curved almost horizontally.

These varieties form the bulk of the Fancy Goldfish interest and include all the colourations and scale patterns previously described. There is even a jet black Goldfish called the Moor.

Typical Fancy varieties are Fantail, Veiltail, Jikin, Ranchu, Ryukin, Wakin, Oranda, Lionhead, Celestial, Bubble-eye and Tosakin and each variety has its own characteristic qualities.

Most of these varieties are not suitable for pond culture and will have lost much of their swimming prowess. Their internal organs will have become cramped through the shaping of the body with the result that some will develop swimming or balance abnormalities.

Other coldwater fishes

Whilst there are many other species of coldwater fish suitable for aquarium culture, recent legislation has made the importing, selling and keeping of such fishes much more difficult, especially those fishes imported from other countries. The reason for this is quite simple: because the fish share the same water conditions in their country that exists here, any imported fish that is set free into our native waters could seriously affect our own native fish stocks, either by predating on them or by breeding at such a fast rate that they are outcompeted for natural food.

At the time of writing, licences are required to be held by both the vendor and purchaser in respect of non-native fishes. Those fishes most affected are many found naturally in North American waters; these include *Pimephales*, *Cyprinella*, *Lepomis*, *Notropis*, and *Umbra*, all very attractive aquarium subjects.

Tropical marine fishes

The range of tropical fishes from the world's coral reefs is extensive and is every way as enthralling as freshwater species.

Although now quite a fully established part of the hobby, marine fishkeeping is still regarded by some as a somewhat specialized interest. For those willing to take up the challenge, there is still much to be discovered in this newest area of fishkeeping, particularly with respect to captive breeding which can play such an important part in conserving stocks in the wild.

The system works in the same way as for freshwater tropical fish with species collected into popular Family groups: Angelfish, Butterflyfish, Clownfish, Damselfish, Surgeons, Tangs, Wrasses, Gobies and so on.

As most marine fish come from very stable water conditions of a very narrow range of specific gravity parameters, in this aspect of fishkeeping there are only compatibility and perhaps feeding problems to deal with when choosing species. Whatever fish you buy will be expected to live in one predetermined set of water conditions – those parameters of the artificial salt water you mix for the aquarium; you will not need to worry about the needs of different species as might be the case for the freshwater aquarium.

However, this compatibility issue should extend to consider what other types of livestock, corals or invertebrates for instance, share the aquarium with the fish. Many of the decorative soft polyp-type corals will be at risk from species such as Butterflyfishes whilst Triggerfishes are quite happy to munch on other invertebrate life.

Suggested fish and plant collections

Within the following suggested community fish collections, whilst we have tried to limit the fish population to definite locations, certain liberties have been taken, especially with respect to the plant recommendations.

Whilst the majority of plants share the same geographic origin as the fish species some, such as *Vallisneria* and *Sagittari*, are included not for their geographical 'correctness' but for their background decorative contributory factor.

A similar discretion should be used in respect of the ubiquitous *Corydoras* Catfish which may, on occasion, seem to have wandered outside its natural South American habitat.

Due to space limitations on one hand, and the added complexity of fish selection on the other, it is regretted that no suggestions are included for a basic tropical marine collection. However, by judicious reading of this guide combined with extra research elsewhere, it would not be too difficult to envisage what might be included in such as collection.

table 3 South American Characins

tank size	fish	plants	water
60 × 38 × 30 cm 24" × 15" × 12"	Neon and/or Cardinal Tetras Lemon Tetras Rosy Tetras Glowlight Tetras *Corydoras* Catfish	*Vallisneria* *Sagittaria* *Amazon Swordplant* *Echinodorus tenellus* *Cabomba* *Hydrocotyle* *Ludwigia* rocks/wood	preferably soft 24–6° Centigrade

table 4 South American Cichlids

tank size	fish	plants	water
60 × 38 × 30 cm 24" × 15" × 12"	Angelfish Apistogramma spp. Laetecara curviceps *Corydoras* Catfish	*Vallisneria* *Sagittaria* *Amazon Swordplant* *Echinodorus tenellus* *Cabomba* *Hydrocotyle* *Ludwigia* rocks/wood	preferably soft 24–6° Centigrade

table 5 African Lake Cichlids

tank size	fish	plants	water
60 × 38 × 30 cm 36" × 15" × 12"	Pseudotropheus spp. Nimbochromis sp. Aulonacara spp. Neolamprologus	rocks large empty shells	very hard 24–6° Centigrade

table 6 Asian Cyprinids

tank size	fish	plants	water
60 × 38 × 30 cm 24" × 15" × 12"	Zebra Danio Harlequin Rasbora Scissortail Rasbora Tiger Barbs Rosy Barbs Ruby Barbs Botia sp.	*Vallisneria* *Saggitaria* *Cryptocoryne* spp. *Hygrophila* *Limnophila* *Microsorium* rocks/wood	moderately soft 24–6° Centigrade

plate 1 aquarium
The complete underwater living picture.

plate 2 Bristol Shubunkin
The Goldfish and its subsequent Fancy Varieties provided the original aquarium fish.

plate 3 Harlequin
The popular Harlequin, *Rasbora heteromorpha*, lays its eggs on the underside of
aquatic plants.

plate 4 Checker Barb
The Checker Barb, *Barbus oligolepis*, is ideally suited to the smaller aquarium.

plate 5 Tinfoil Barb
The Tinfoil Barb, *Barbus schwanenfeldi*, can grow to over 30 cm.

plate 6 Silver Shark
The fast swimming Silver Shark, *Balantiocheilus melanopterus*, needs a large aquarium.

plate 7 Diamond Tetra
The iridescent speckles on the flanks of the Diamond Tetra, *Moenkhausia pittieri*, are best seen under a little side-lighting.

plate 8 Cardinal Tetra
The Cardinal Tetra, *Paracheirodon axelrodi*, can be easily distinguished from the Neon Tetra as it has the bright red colouration running the whole length of the body.

plate 9 Emperor Tetra
The male Emperor Tetra, *Nematobrycon palmeri*, is easily recognized by the central extension ray to the caudal fin.

plate 10 Bleeding Heart Tetra
Bleeding Heart Tetras, *Hyphessobrycon erythrostigma*, are often nervous fish when first introduced.

plate 11 Angelfish
The Angelfish, *Pterophyllum scalare*, is now available in other colour varieties than this standard silver patterning.

plate 12 Discus
This variety of Discus, *Symphysodon sp*, is far removed from the original colouration of the natural wild species.

plate 13 Thomasi
The modestly-sized African Cichlid, *Anomalochromis thomasi*, is another excellent candidate for the smaller aquarium.

plate 14 group of Rift Lake Cichlids
Rift Valley Lake Cichlids prefer rocky aquariums and hard water.

plate 15 Lyretail Swordtail
This Swordtail, *Xiphorus helleri*, is clearly an aquarium-developed strain.

plate 16 Gold Sailfin Molly
This Gold Sailfin Molly is an aquarium-developed variety.

plate 17 Guppy
Due to its incredible reproduction rate the Guppy, *Poecilia reticulata*, is also known as the Millions Fish.

plate 18 Variatus Platy
This Platy, *Xiphophorus variatus*, looks like a 'stretched' version of its smaller relation, *X.maculatus*.

plate 19 Dwarf Gourami
For its size the Dwarf Gourami, *Colisa lalia*, can be remarkably aggressive during its breeding period.

plate 20 Moonlight Gourami
The tiny burnished scales of the Moonlight Gourami, *Trichogaster microlepis*, gave rise to the specific part of its taxonomic name, which means 'tiny scaled'.

plate 21 Siamese Fighting Fish
Everyone recognises the Siamese Fighting Fish, *Betta splendens*.

plate 22 Sparkling Gourami
The small Sparkling Gourami, *Trichopsis pumilus*, is a tiny jewel of a fish which does well in a tank just with its own kind.

plate 23 Nothobranchius
Sadly, most Killifish are only known by their scientific names. This one is
Nothobranchius foerschi, but looks good all the same.

plate 24 Pearlfish
The colouration of the Argentinian Pearlfish, *Cynolebias nigripinnis*, is reminiscent of a
starry night.

plate 25 Melanotaenia sp
This rainbow fish will develop a deeper body with adulthood.

plate 26 Melanotaenia maccullochi
This rainbow fish, *Melanotaenia maccullochi*, is an old favourite amongst the many
new species now seen.

plate 27 Melanotaenia praecox
Like all Rainbow fishes, *Melanotaenia praecox* has two separate dorsal fins.

plate 28 Melanotaenia splendida australis
Melanotaenia spedida australis is not impartial to hard water and looks great in a shoal.

plate 29 Synodontis angelicus
This near adult *Synodontis angelicus* has lost its violet colouration as a youngster but will still retain its white spots for a time.

plate 30 Corydoras sp
Whilst they are excellent scavengers, *Corydoras* catfish should be kept for their own sake, not just as aquarium refuse collectors.

plate 31 Clown Loach
Loaches are gregarious fish, so this Clown Loach, *Chromobotia macracantha* needs room for its tankmates – it grows big too.

plate 32 Botia striata
If you have snails in your aquarium, Loaches such as this *Botia striata*, should clear them out.

table 7 Asian Labyrinths

tank size	fish	plants	water
60 × 38 × 30 cm 24" × 15" × 12"	Dwarf Gourami Leeri Gourami Three-spot Gourami Opaline Gourami Thicklip Gourami Botia sp.	*Vallisneria* *Saggitaria* *Cryptocoryne* spp. *Hygrophila* *Limnophila* *Microsorium* rocks/wood	moderately soft 24–6° Centigrade

table 8 Central American livebearers

tank size	fish	plants	water
60 × 38 × 30 cm 24" × 15" × 12"	Wagtail Platy Swordtails Guppies Mollies *Corydoras* Catfish	*Vallisneria* *Saggitaria* *Cryptocoryne* spp. *Hygrophila* *Limnophila* *Microsorium* *Riccia* rocks/wood	moderately soft 24–6° Centigrade

table 9 Goldfish

tank size	fish	plants	water
90 × 38 × 30 cm 36" × 15" × 12"	Common Goldfish Bristol/London Shubunkins Fantail Pearlscale	*Vallisneria* *Myriophyllum* *Hornwort*	n/a cold water

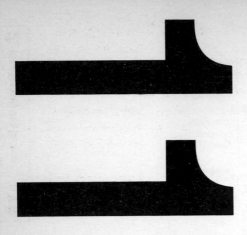

introducing the fish

In this chapter you will learn:
- getting the fish home safely
- introducing the first fish into the aquarium
- dealing with new, extra fish.

The fish will have had a fairly stressful time being caught from the dealer's tank, placed in a plastic bag (hopefully further placed in a dark, brown paper bag) and transported to your home. You should therefore introduce the fish into its new aquarium with as little extra disturbance as possible.

It is most likely that you will have purchased your first fishes from a local aquatic outlet, and so there should be little variance in water quality between that of the dealer's supply and your domestic supply.

The only thing that will have varied since the fish was purchased will be the temperature of the water. Exposing a fish to any sudden change of condition, even temperature, should be avoided.

If, however, your journey home is likely to be a lengthy one or it is to be made during the winter, then some precautions should be taken to prevent the fish becoming chilled. Any heat insulated container can be used even, paradoxically, a cool-box. As you will be hopefully a continuing customer at the aquatic store for some appreciable time to come, it would be worth getting hold of one of the polystyrene container that the fish are transported in to your dealer; he may consider letting you have one as an incentive for future custom!

To equalize the water temperature in the plastic transportation bag to that of your aquarium, all that is required is to float the bag in the aquarium for 20 minutes or so.

Some people advocate that the bag is opened and that some aquarium water is gradually added so as to acclimatize the fish to the water quality too, but others believe that the amounts of water involved will not make any difference.

At the end of the temperature equalization period, gently tip over the plastic bag and let the fish swim out into their new home. Again, some people avoid adding too much 'shop water' from the bag into the aquarium but the amount involved is almost negligible against the total volume of the aquarium.

It may be a good idea to transfer fish into the aquarium under subdued lighting conditions.

Don't worry if the fish dive for the nearest clump of plants or hide behind the rocks. It will take them a little time to accustom themselves to their new surroundings. Eeventually, they will come out, even though it may take a pinch of food to coax them out.

This introduction process should be used each time new fish are added, even to a quarantine tank (see also p. 109). Giving a small amount of food to fish already in the tank, to distract their attention from the newcomers being introduced, is a ploy often recommended.

12

what's on the menu?

In this chapter you will learn:
- what to feed, and to which fish
- culturing livefoods
- caring for fish during the holidays.

Feeding aquarium fish should not be seen just as a daily chore of opening up the aquarium hood and tipping in something out of a tub. Although it can be as simple as that, the dietary needs of your fish should be considered a little more deeply if they are to thrive to their full potential.

Quantity

It should be said that, right from the start, fish do not need as much food as we think they do. Terrestrial animals consume food to build up energy, body muscle and to conserve their body temperature; fish only need food for energy and to build up their body. Their body temperature corresponds to, and is governed by, that of the surrounding water.

Perversely, food can also be dangerous to fish. Not because they end up over-weight but, because if they are over-fed, any food they do not eat (or food that they do eat but not necessarily digest) pollutes the aquarium water. It is an old fishkeeping adage that more fish are killed by kindness (over-feeding) than by neglect.

The basic rule for feeding is to only give enough food at any one time so that it is totally eaten within a couple of minutes. Of course, fish soon learn that food comes in through the top of the tank and will tend to congregate expectantly if they catch a glimpse of their owner through the front glass. This should not be taken as a sign that the fish are hungry, and new fishkeepers should brace themselves against the natural reaction to give the fish food every time they go near the tank. You can see where the danger lies if you don't tell the rest of the family that you have fed the fish.

Over-feeding not only pollutes the tank and wastes money, but it also builds up nutrients in the water to encourage algae problems. Make it a case of 'feed the fish, not the algae.'

What to feed

Everything you need to feed fish is available at the aquatic store, as fish food manufacturers have not only thoroughly researched what fishes actually require nutritonally but have this produced the edible products. Any fish, whether carnivore, herbivore or omnivore can rest assured it won't starve in your aquarium. But it's not just a matter of producing something that is acceptable to the fish; the 'design' of fish food is a lot more complicated than that.

Foods aren't just manufactured in the required 'flavours' or recipes but also fortified with the necessary vitamins and immuno-reinforcers to ensure the fish remain healthy and are able to fight off disease.

It is important that the food make up suits the fish at every stage of its development. Hence, foods for fast-growing fry will contain more protein that that required for near adult fish who may have finished their growth period.

Digestibility, particularly for fish where water temperatures vary throughout the year, is also a consideration. Pond fish, for example, require an easily digestible food for when they emerge from their winter torpor and also in autumn when the water cools down and their demand for food lessens. Any food laying undigested in the fish's gut can decompose and cause problems.

It is the aim of the food manufacturers to make sure that as much of the food is utilized for the fish's needs and that as little waste material as possible is produced. This reduces the bio-load on the aquarium's filtration system which, in turn, reduces maintenance time for the fishkeeper.

Commercially-produced foods are also tailored to suit the various feeding methods of fish. Typical fish food formats now include flake, granular, extruded sticks, wafers, crisps, paste, liquid, pellet, tablet, freeze-dried and frozen options. Why so many formats?

table 3 feeding information

fish group	feeding zone	preferred diet	suitable food (see key below)
Barbs	all levels	omnivorous	A, B, C, P, T
Catfish	bottom	omnivorous, some vegetarian	B F
Characins	all levels	omnivorous, some carnivorous	A, B, C, T
Cichlids	all levels	omnivorous, some vegetarian	A, B, C, P, T A, C, P
Danios	mid, upper	omnivorous	A, C
Goldfish	all levels	omnivorous	A, B, E, P
Gouramies	mid, upper	omnivorous some vegetarian	A, B, C, P
Killifish	upper	omnivorous	A, B, C
livebearers	all levels	omnivorous	A, B, C, P, T
Loaches	bottom	carnivorous	B
Rasboras	mid, upper	omnivorous	A, B, C
Tetras	all levels	omnivorous	A, B, C, T

Key to foods types:

A = flake	E = extruded sticks	H = liquid
B = granular	F = wafers	P = pellet
C = crisps	G = paste	T = tablet

The various formats available are linked to how fishes feed. Foods must stay in the fish's vicinity long enough for the fish to take it. Its 'taste' may also attract the fish to it, say, when the tank is in darkness.

Another requirement is that the food particle must also be of the right size for the age of the fish. Liquid foods of extremely small particle size are not only ideal for very young fish but a marine version of this is useful when it comes to feeding sedentary animals such as corals.

Other foods

But fish in nature don't have access to tubs of food, you might say, surely they live on natural foods? It is quite true to say that, for instance, in the marine world the favourite food for fish is fish, or other sea-living animals. Manufacturers use shellfish, crustaceans and small fishes not just as ingredients but they also freeze them straight from capture.

Anyone who has a rain butt in the garden will be familiar with the colonies of insect larvae that live in the water at certain times of year. These can be netted out and make excellent fish foods, especially for bringing fish into breeding condition. Other larvae found in the rain butt or other bodies of standing water, may include Bloodworm, the larvae of the Gnat or Midge, which also makes an excellent food.

Another natural living fish food is *Daphnia*, the Water Flea, that lives in duck ponds and other small bodies of water which contain no fish. A netful of *Daphnia* will also capture other microscopic forms of aquatic life, all of which are relished by aquarium fish. The only precaution to take when collecting such foods is to avoid introducing certain large insect larvae, such as Dragonfly larvae, Water Beetles, Water Boatman, Water Scorpions and the like into the aquarium as these will predate on very small fishes.

It is hard to imagine where fish could possibly have acquired the taste for earthworms, but they accept them most readily, even though it may not a pleasant job chopping them up small enough.

Worm foods, relished by all aquarium fish, can be cultured quite easily. The size of the food depends on the species of worm being raised. Apart from Micro-eels (microscopic eels raised in a sugary liquid), the smallest worm normally cultured is Micro-worm and successive 'size' increases are provided by Grindal-Worm and White-worm. Each of these worms are cultured in small containers and fed with some kind of cereal food. Micro-worms remain in a semi-liquid culture but

Grindal- and White-worms are usually raised in a drier, peat-based litter and fed with cereal food and pieces of bread respectively. White-worms generally prefer slighter cooler conditions than Grindal-worms.

A common characteristic in culturing these foods is the first sign of a deteriorating culture – the smell! You soon learn to gauge the life of each culture and so take a small sample at this time to begin a new culture.

Raising young fry successfully relies on having a constant supply of suitable food available 24 hours a day. A very popular food for this purpose is Brine Shrimp. This is a tiny Shrimp, *Artemia salina*, living in salt water, usually near salt flats; famous sources are in Utah and San Francisco Bay in the USA. The eggs of these shrimps are harvested and stored in dry conditions. When immersed in salt water, the eggs hatch and the newly-hatched shrimp, known as *nauplii*, make an excellent first food for baby fish. One advantage of using this food is that although coming from an aquatic source, it is completely disease-free, unlike other aquatic foods that may be captured in freshwater, fish-inhabited locations.

Hatching the eggs is straightforward. An inverted plastic bottle has its bottom removed and an airline inserted through the stopper. The bottle is filled with salt water – a strength of about 1½ tablespoonfuls of sea salt (natural salt) per litre of water – or with an SG of 1.018 if you are using a hydrometer and ½ teaspoon of egg added.

Air

figure 23 an inverted plastic bottle is used for hatching shrimps

With aeration, and a water temperature of around 80°F, the shrimps should hatch in around 24 hours. Disconnect the aeration and let the contents settle. The empty eggshells should fall to the bottom leaving the shrimps swimming in the water, from where they can be netted out using a very fine net. The shrimps should be rinsed to remove the salt and then fed to the fish.

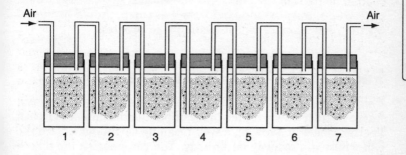

figure 24 sequential hatchers

When raising a large number of fry, it is advisable to have several cultures of shrimp hatching sequentially so that the food supply doesn't run out. Each bottle's culture can be started a day or two apart. The diagram shows sequential hatchers fed from one air-pump.

Vegetarian-minded fish may present apparent feeding problems. Usually such fish are introduced deliberately into the aquarium to deal with growths of unwanted algae. Alternative green foods are blanched lettuce, sliced courgettes and shelled tinned peas. Of course, it is possible to farm your own algae in a separate well-lit aquarium or, if you have a number of tanks, you can use regular algae scrapings from them to feed the fish.

Feeding marine fish follows the same practices and, as in the freshwater aquarium, there are vegetarian species, such as Tangs and Surgeonfish. In tanks containing such species, lush algae growths should be encouraged or algae grown in separate tanks fed to them. One practical tip would be to introduce algae-covered rocks from other tanks into the Tangs' tank for them to clean. Rotating the supply of algae-covered rocks not only keeps the rocks clean but also satisfies the need for green matter in these fishes' diets.

In reef tanks, where there may be sedentary invertebrates such as soft corals present, these animals cannot chase after their food as can fish and so the food must be presented to them.

Emulsified shellfish and/or specialized liquid foods can be given to individual coral heads using a turkey baster. Alternatively, where the aquarium is fitted with several powerheads to provide water currents, these should be left running to distribute the food to all parts of the tank. Any filtration system, which would otherwise extract the food before it was eaten, should be turned off for a few minutes whilst feeding is in progress.

Feeding the fish during the holidays

This is a question often asked by new fishkeepers. We have seen learned earlier how over-feeding can pollute the tank and herein lies the danger of allowing a well-meaning neighbour to feed the fish whilst you're away on holiday. You can imagine the scene:

'Here's a tub of food for the fish, whilst we're away.' 'OK. I'll pop in every day and feed them, no problem. Have a good holiday!'

Fast forward to the fishkeeper's return, only to find the whole tub of food has been used! Thankfully the fish are fine but there's a deep layer of uneaten food on the tank floor.

The moral here is obvious – if you trust someone to feed the fish in your absence make sure they know how to do it correctly or you can make up small packets of daily (or every other day) feeding portions so that they can't go wrong.

What most experienced fishkeepers have found is that, providing the fish have previously been well cared for and fed normally prior to the holiday period, leaving them unfed works just as well and you avoid potential tank pollution worries. You may well return home to a cleaner tank!

13 routine maintenance

In this chapter you will learn:
- regular maintenance tasks
- changing water, cleaning filters
- handling and transporting fish.

Although the aquarium is often regarded as a slice of underwater life, unlike the river or stream it is not self-maintaining and requires regular support from the fishkeeper. The fish depends on its owner for everything – food, light, water quality and equipment reliability. Failure to carry out simple maintenance tasks is a recipe for disaster, not only for the fish themselves but for the hobby too as it may lose another follower. Maintenance doesn't have to be a chore; compared to the many hours that you'll spend gazing into the aquarium's depths the proportion of time spent on maintenance is hardly measurable.

The following chart outlines the most important items to be checked. (NB: SG, ammonia, nitrite and nitrate checks must especially be carried out during the maturation period.)

table 11 routine maintenance tasks

task	weekly		monthly		periodically		if fish behaviour is abnormal	
	fresh	marine	fresh	marine	fresh	Marine	fresh	marine
check number of fish	*	*	*	*	*	*		
water								
temperature					*	*	*	*
pH							*	*
SG		*		*				*
ammonia	*	*					*	*
nitrite	*	*					*	*
nitrate	*	*					*	*
partial water change			*	*				
filter								
clean impeller housing					*			
clean and/or replace medium					*			

task	weekly		monthly		periodically		if fish behaviour is abnormal	
	fresh	marine	fresh	marine	fresh	marine	fresh	marine
replace carbon and phosphate removing medium					*			
empty protein skimmer cup		*						
clean interior of protein skimmer of residue						*		
rake over substrate					*	*		
plants								
remove dead plants					*			
prune rampant growth					*			
remove algae from front glass					*	*		
general								
clean air-pump valves and filter						*		
renew lamps					*	*		
clean cover glass	*	*						
remove salt deposits from hood and tank exterior						*		
clean water pump impellers						*		

Aquarium management

The main purpose of the following notes is not only to outline the necessary tasks to keep the aquarium in good running order but also to do so in such a manner so as to avoid exposing the fish to undue stress in the process. It is not a rigid timetable to be followed slavishly. Fish have to fit into our pattern of living but we should try to ensure that we consider their requirements as much as, if not more than, our own.

One good rule in fishkeeping is to minimize how often you put your hands in the tank. This will interfere with the tank's natural routine, so follow the another key piece of advice – 'If it ain't broke, don't fix it!'

In tropical climes, fish are subjected to a regular routine with hours of daylight and darkness well defined. You can simulate this by using a timer to switch on and off the aquarium lights accordingly if you so wish.

Where the daylight hours vary according to season, the act of switching the aquarium lights on and off at set times may stress the fish if they are plunged from darkness into brightness (and vice versa) too suddenly. To prevent this, when the mornings and evenings are dark switch on a room light *ahead* of the aquarium light in the morning and off *after* the aquarium light in the evening.

Where extra aquarium lights have been fitted, you can arrange separate timing switches to switch on, and turn off, various combinations of fluorescent tubes to simulate dawn, midday and dusk conditions.

Partial water changes should be done as smoothly as possible. The replacement water should be at the same temperature as that of the water being removed and of the same composition. Remember to add the correct dose of dechlorinator to the replacement water before using it in the aquarium.

The amount of water removed at each change is generally between 10–20 per cent; the frequency of change depends on how 'dirty' the inhabitants of the tank are – large, heavy feeding Cichlids produce more waste than just a few decorative Tetras.

It is generally agreed that 'little and often' is more beneficial than a large water change not so frequently, although remember that too many frequent water changes might not give either the fish or the filtration time to settle down.

How to change water

The easiest method is to simply siphon out the required amount of water into a bucket and top up the tank with fresh water.

Siphoning from just above the substrate surface will remove any settled detritus at the same time. To remove any fine silt that has accumulated within the substrate, the use of a 'gravel washer' is recommended; this removes the silt along with the water without removing any of the substrate material in the process.

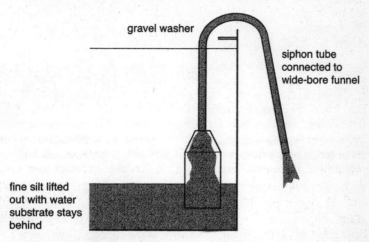

gravel washer

siphon tube connected to wide-bore funnel

fine silt lifted out with water substrate stays behind

figure 26 gravel washer operation

Keeping the glass clean

This is an obvious chore of course, as you will want to be able to see your fish as clearly as you can. It's probably only necessary to clean off algae from the inside of the front glass; the other interior walls of the tank will provide useful grazing grounds for any vegetarian species of fish in your collection.

It is important to use the correct material to clean off the algae: glass and acrylic panels need different types of material if you want to avoid scratching of the surface. Permanent algae-scrapers can be mounted on the tank. These magnetically-coupled devices allow you to move the exterior portion across the glass whilst the other roughened internal part follows, removing the algae without the need to get your hands wet – there is even a design that floats up to the surface if magnetic contact is lost.

Often overlooked is the cover glass. This also needs to be kept scrupulously clean if all the available light is to be utilized by plants in the aquarium. Additionally, the fluorescent tubes need replacing anually. Check the waterproof fluorescent tube end caps, or similar sealing collars, when changing lamps.

Cleaning filters

Murky water prevents us from seeing the fish and also deprives plants of photosynthesis-inducing light. Periodically, the sponge filter medium should be cleaned relieving it of any suspended materials it has removed from the water.

Sponge filter media also acts as a biological filter to some degree and it is vital that the washing process does not destroy the nitrifying bacteria within the sponge. Most fishkeepers wash out the filter medium in some aquarium water to prevent this happening. Another way to minimize the risk is that where there are several layers of sponge material in the filter, you should only rinse out a proportion of them at any one time; this will help to maintain a colony of bacteria within the filter medium too.

Don't forget to check out the filter motor assembly, particularly the impeller. Over time, this will become coated with organic slime and could lose some of its efficiency. It is a simple operation to open up the assembly, wipe off the slime from the impeller and cylindrical magnetic rotor and replace.

Whilst you are working with an outside filter, it makes good preventative sense to check that any hose clips have not become loose. This will prevent leaks and potential floods.

There's a filter that most people either forget or don't even know exists – the filter in the base of the air-pump. This felt pad cleans the air before it is pumped into the aquarium, so don't neglect it. Still with the air-pump, any lessening of output may be due to sticking valves in its output chamber or a split diaphragm. Should you need to investigate, then always switch off the pump before opening it as there will be electrical connections inside.

A protein skimmer will lose efficiency if there is a build-up of organic matter or algae in its internal surfaces. Disconnect periodically and give it a good clean.

Keeping a clean tank

Take care to keep the tank clean. Use an aquarium 'vacuum cleaner' to pick up debris, uneaten food, dead plant material, etc. from the substrate if necessary. Any materials that decompose in the tank will consume vital oxygen and also encourage algae growth.

If the aquarium forms part of a piece of furniture, check the cabinet for lifting veneers due to possible condensation and, in the case of marine aquariums, wipe off any salt deposits that may have built up; this is bound to happen, especially where there is an external filtration pump system housed in the cupboard under the aquarium.

Handling fish

Catching fish can be just as stressful for the fishkeeper as for the fish (sometimes more so!) so go about it methodically.

You will find that using two nets is useful; holding one still and guiding the fish with the other often brings an early success.

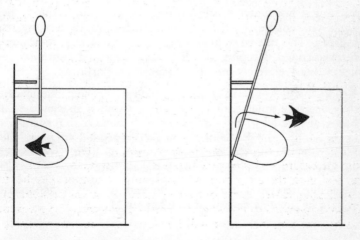

figure 26 avoid escape routes by ensuring net handles bend around the glass shelf

Make sure net handles are bent to go around the glass shelf at the top of the tank, so that there are no escape routes around the net when it is pressed up against the glass. When catching fish that have sharp spines and/or long delicate fins, it may be better to chase them into a large plastic bag or large jar to avoid snagging in nets or damaging their fins. If handling marine fish with toxin-filled spines, make sure you wear rubber gloves.

Transporting fish to Shows

You must ensure that fish are not stressed when transporting them to fish Shows where they will need to arrive looking their best.

Fish are normally exhibited in small all-glass containers and it is best that they travel to and from the Show in their respective Show tanks. Being small, a number of these tanks (with suitable polystyrene packing between them) can be packed in a polystyrene container; you can get these containers from your aquatic dealer as they are those that fish are in when they arrive from abroad.

Travelling in their own tanks, in water they are accustomed to, will avoid stressing the fish although you should take some extra water with you to compensate for any spillages. This way you will not have to use 'strange' water as supplied at the destination.

Packing a hot water bottle in the box, or using modern 'heat pads' will ensure the fish stay warm during any lengthy road journey. The use of a heat insulated polystyrene container is recommended. Keeping the fish in a darkened container also keeps them relatively inactive during transportation.

Goldfish will not need quite so much pampering but, because they are that much larger than most tropical species they are best transported in five-litre sized polythene 'painters buckets' using a clip-on lid. Again, it is recommended to paint these buckets black (on the outside!) to exclude light. Goldfish can equally well be carried in a black plastic bag.

Releasing fish into a tank at the end of any transportation should be done as described in Chapter 11.

14

in sickness and in health

In this chapter you will learn:
- preventing fish diseases
- recognizing fish diseases
- how to treat fish diseases.

Even in the best managed aquarium things can go wrong and, whilst we would rather not admit to it, disease sometimes strikes. It is usually the result of a change in the aquarium's environments: an extra fish can put a stress on the whole aquarium, disease may be inadvertently introduced with a new species of fish or plant or an equipment breakdown can put the whole system in jeopardy. But we should think positively. Rather than believe it won't ever happen, we should either take steps to prevent things going wrong or at least be prepared to deal with them if they do.

Prevention

Prevention is the best form of defence against illness. It is imperative that only healthy fish are introduced into the aquarium, so be on your guard right from the outset.

When looking at potential purchases make sure that:

- The fish is swimming effortlessly and can maintain its chosen position in the water.
- Colours are intense and patterns well-defined.
- It is free from split fins, wounds, sores or other skin abrasions.
- Its fins are erect – in freshwater fishes, folded fins are a sign that the fish is not happy.
- It is not behaving abnormally – hiding away from other fish or occupying the wrong place in the tank for its species.
- There are no dead fish in the tank, even though they may be of a different species to the one you are interested in.
- The fish is feeding – ask the dealer about this, especially with respect to marine species.
- You understand how to care for the fish, especially if it needs special water conditions or a special diet.
- You know how big the fish will grow, and whether it is (or will be) compatible with further purchases or already existing stock.

If any of the above criteria cannot be fulfilled, then the best policy is to leave the fish in the shop rather than risk putting your aquarium at risk.

Even if your intended purchase is quite healthy and you make the purchase it is still expedient to treat it with caution.

Quarantining

Quarantining new stock is always worth the time and effort.

Ideally, the quarantine tank should mirror the same water conditions as that in your main aquarium so that transferring fish from one to the other is stress free.

The quarantine tank need not be too large, as you'll only be using it for two or three fish at a time at most. It can also be used as a hospital tank (for the treatment of disease of individual fish), breeding tank when not required or as quarantine accommodation for new stock.

To cut the risk of any disease lurking in the quarantine tank it need not be furnished to any great degree. There is no need for any substrate or plants. To give the fish some sense of security, lay a medium-sized plastic flowerpot on its side on the tank floor; fish can then hide behind it or in it as they so desire.

A small internal power filter may be used but remove any carbon filter medium from it should you need to medicate the tank. Remember that medications often consume oxygen, so it's a good idea to provide extra aeration at this time.

Use a cover glass and only a low-wattage light. This will help to keep the fish subdued. Fish should be kept in the quarantine tank for at least 10–14 days, during which time any latent disease should manifest itself. If disease does strike then the fish can be immediately treated in the quarantine tank with the appropriate remedy.

Before transferring fish to the main aquarium at the end of their quarantine period, if you had occasion to treat the tank for disease then you should at least carry out a partial water change and/or replace the carbon filter medium in the filter to remove any medication from the water.

Recognizing disease

The key to diagnosing diseases in the aquarium is to develop a keen sense of observation. Only by continually observing your fish, and getting to know their normal habits and behaviour, can you build up enough information to know when something is wrong with a fish.

To a certain extent, a similar watch on the tank's water conditions can also reveal something is amiss. A sudden deviation in the pH for instance may point towards a dead fish decomposing behind a rock that may have escaped your notice. If the water-flow from the filter's return has diminished then it's a sure sign that the filter needs cleaning!

In today's centrally-heated accommodations it's quite easy not to notice that the aquarium heater isn't working. All these factors can lead to fish becoming stressed and succumbing to infection.

Fish ailments

Fish ailments can range from their equivalent of a common cold to some debilitating infection that is beyond treatment. Diseases fall into two groups, those that have early external visible symptoms and those that don't. The problem with the latter type is that by the time the fish's behaviour or eventual general appearance tells you something is wrong, it's usually too late to effect a cure.

White Spot

This is the disease every freshwater aquarium gets at one time or another. Its name is accurately descriptive, the infected fish being covered with tiny white spots. Breathing may be affected as the disease spreads to the delicate gill membranes whilst those on the skin cause irritation that the fish tries to alleviate by scratching itself against firm aquarium objects such as rocks or the substrate.

Caused by the parasite *Ichthyophthirius multifilis*, the illness has a cyclical life span. From the spots on the fish, cysts fall to the bottom of the aquarium to rise again as spores seeking another host. It is in this free-swimming stage that treatment must be applied. The whole aquarium may be treated, avoiding the need for a hospital tank to be set up. Proprietary remedies work well.

The marine equivalent is caused by the parasite *Cryptocaryon irritans* but the freshwater copper-based remedies cannot be used in the main aquarium due to their high toxicity to invertebrate life in the tank and because the copper will be absorbed by calcium, magnesium and living rock before it effects a cure. Copper cures can be used in a bare hospital tank

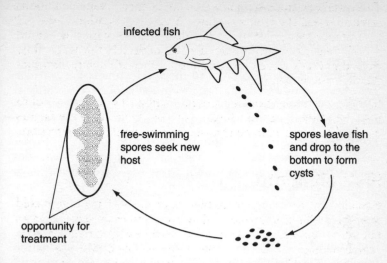

figure 27 White Spot life cycle

and, if all the fish to be treated are kept in this tank for at least a month the main aquarium should be free of any spores or cysts when the fish are returned. Other remedies include hyposalination – keeping the fish in a treatment tank at lower SG levels – and transferring them every other day to a freshly set up clean aquarium.

Velvet

A similar disease to White Spot is Velvet. Caused by the parasite *Oodinium* (now *Piscinoodinium*) *pillularis*, the symptomatic spots on the fish's body are far smaller, giving the impression of being 'dusty'. Again the fish's attempts to alleviate the disease are scratching, increased breathing and maybe some rusty patches of colour appearing.

Treatment is to use a salt bath in a darkened tank (the parasitic spores often photosynthesize) coupled with a few degrees rise in temperature, if the fish can tolerate it. Trypaflavine is another alternative remedy, again with an increase in temperature.

Amyloodinium ocellatum is responsible for Marine Velvet. Treatments include copper and freshwater dips.

Gill and skin flukes

These, literally, irritating ailments are caused by two separate, yet remarkably similar-sounding worm parasites – *Dactylogyrus* and *Gyrodactylus*. These creatures are armed with hooks by which they attach themselves to their unfortunate hosts which are soon debilitated by their blood-sucking attentions. Listlessness, loss of energy, faded colour and difficulties in breathing are all symptomatic of an attack by these parasites.

Initial treatment in the hospital tank should involve a 25 per cent water change before moving on to recognized remedies such as formalin and organophophorus-based treatments, both of which should be handled with care.

Fin Rot

Not so much a disease as rather a secondary illness. Where a fin becomes split, it provides an excellent location for disease to invade. It is usually in poorly-maintained aquariums where water conditions are well below what is recommended and the tank's overall hygiene has been neglected that such secondary diseases flourish. Transferring the fish to better surroundings usually affects a cure.

Fungus

Caused by the fungal mould *Saprolegnia*, Fungus is again a secondary invader after the fish has been attacked by a parasite, has an open wound and is being kept in less than perfect water conditions. The disease looks like tufts of greyish cotton wool attending the affected area. Salt baths are beneficial as are proprietary treatments allied to improved aquarium hygiene.

Mouth Fungus

Although apparently sharing similar visible description to Fungus, this particular ailment is not caused by the same fungal mould but by a bacterium *Flavobacterium columnare* (formerly *Flexibacter columnaris*). Enouraged by poor aquarium conditions, the disease should respond to treatment with antibacterial remedies.

Neon Tetra Disease

Named after the Neon Tetra in which it was first found, it is caused by *Pleistophora hyphessobryconis*. Symptoms are fading of colour on the fish together with subsequent wastage of muscles and loss of swimming ability with death being the inevitable outcome. All affected fish should be removed and destroyed as there is no reliable remedy.

Dropsy

This debilitating disease is not a pretty sight. The scales stand out almost at right angles from the body which has become distended through the build up of fluid internally. Gouramies seem particularly prone but there is no consensus as to the actual cause or whether it is as contagious as some believe. Affected fish should be removed for risk that other fish may eat their dead bodies and so contract the disease. Possible effective treatments include anti-internal bacterial remedies. Experimental drawing off of the bodily fluid with a syringe is not to be recommended.

Hole-in-the-Head

Unfortunately, this disease is as distressing as its name implies with tiny holes appearing on the head and along the lateral line (where it is called Lateral Line Erosion). Certain Cichlids, such as *Discus* and *Uaru*, seem prone to this as are many marine fish. The cause is a parasite, *Hexamita*, but there are many opinions as to what triggers an attack from blaming poor conditions, stress and even carbon in filter. Remedies containing Metronidazole are said to be effective.

Shimmying

Sometimes you see a fish, especially Mollies, standing on the spot and gently swaying from side to side. According to some, this is not a disease, or anything affecting their balance, but merely their reaction to cool temperatures as raising the water temperature usually makes them stop doing it. Other sources feel that this may be the onset of symptoms caused by a massive invasion of many pathogens and bacteria, requiring at least a salt bath and perhaps the use of a proprietary remedy.

Swimming Disorder

Where a fish cannot maintain a definite position in the water, for instance, bobbing up or down, or tumbling head over heels when swimming then this is due to a malfunction with the swim-bladder. It is not an uncommon ailment in Fancy Goldfish, where the internal organs have been forced into restricted space due to the desire for a certain body shape on the part of the fish breeder.

Sometimes other internal disorders such as indigestion, can have a knock-on effect on the swim-bladder. Here, the remedy is to feed a wide and varied diet (including live foods) and to add a light laxative, such as Epsom Salts, to the food to clear any digestive tract congestion.

Diagnosing and treating disease

As with quarantining, the course of treatment must be thorough and also well documented.

Don't jump to conclusions. An example of this might be the following scenario: fish are panting at the surface. Obviously an oxygen deficiency, but where? If adding extra aeration doesn't relieve the situation then there may be enough oxygen in the water, but the fish cannot access it because of a parasitic gill infection. So the next step is to examine the fish's gills. Depending on the problem, there are two options open for methods of administering treatment. Treatments can be carried out collectively in the main aquarium, say, for curing a disease that all the fish have contracted; or a single fish, say, suffering from a wound or sore, can be individually treated in a separate hospital tank.

With regard to the use of treatments, when adding treatments to the hospital tank always remove any carbon from the filter first, as the carbon will remove the medication before it can affect a cure. Some remedies may be light sensitive, so it is a good practice to keep the hospital tank under subdued lighting conditions.

Always follow the manufacturer's instructions as accurately as possible. You will need to know the exact water volume capacity of the hospital tank (or tank to be treated). Never be tempted to add a bit more medication 'to be on the safe side'; over-dosing can be lethal, whilst under-dosing can be ineffective.

Never go on to a different treatment immediately (if the first remedy tried failed to work) without returning the water conditions in the hospital tank to normal first. This is to avoid an accumulation of remedies in the tank, as they may react together to create a toxic situation. A further reason for this is that should a subsequent remedy prove to work, how can you be sure it was the last used remedy or a combination of all remedies you may have used?

Make sure that all equipment used in and around the hospital tank never comes into contact with any equipment used for other tanks. This will reduce the risk of cross-infections.

Should the worst happen

The fishkeeper's responsibility to the environment also includes disposing of any dead fish. Flushing down the toilet is not acceptable as pathogens could re-enter the native water system. Incineration is preferred with burial another alternative.

Also in mind the possibilities of contaminating the water system when disposing of water during routine maintenance, should any fish in the aquarium appear diseased. Scattering the water over a wide area in the garden should ensure it 'degrades' as fast as possible before it seeps through the soil to find its natural way back to the water system.

15
the patter
of tiny fins

In this chapter you will learn:
- how fish breed
- breeding fish in the aquarium
- fish breeding case histories.

Probably the last thing on your mind when you bought your first aquarium was that the fish you got for it would breed. Most new fishkeepers aren't aware that either their fish will breed or how they actually go about it. But, it has to be said, that many fish will breed in captivity despite the conditions in which they're being kept – what better compliment could a fishkeeper wish for?

Most people understand that fish breed by laying eggs (spawn) but, once immersed in the fish hobby, you will find that it's a bit more complicated than that. It's how the egg develops that differentiates one group of fishes from another, and there are fascinating variations on this theme along the way too.

Methods of reproduction

Aquarium fish are regarded as belonging to two main groups: **egg-layers** and **livebearers**.

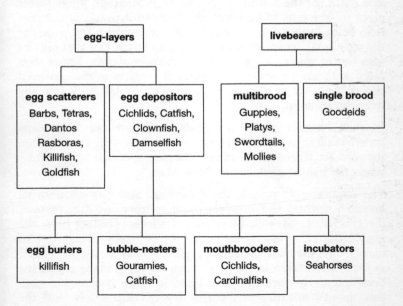

figure 28 fish reproduction methods

The majority of fishes are egg-layers. The female fish, under stimulation by the male, expels eggs, which the male fish then fertilizes. Different species have different ways of going this.

Egg-scattering fish are a promiscuous lot with males and females spawning almost at will with no sense of responsibility for the subsequent fertilized eggs, many of which will be eaten by other fish if not by the parents themselves.

Egg-depositing fish are a bit more careful, with the eggs being laid in a specific area chosen by the fish – it might be on or under a plant leaf, on a rock, on the ceiling inside a rocky cave or placed beneath a floating nest of bubbles built by the male fish. After all this preparation it should not come as a surprise that the proud parents also tend to their newly-hatched offspring defending them against any would-be predator.

Some fish go to extraordinary lengths to protect their young or even to avoid the species being lost through natural disasters. Where else would the throat cavity of one of their parents be a safe place for the fertilized eggs to be incubated? What better place for the eggs to be when the riverbed dries up in summer than being buried deep in the mud at the bottom? The prize for the most imaginative protection must go to the fish that lays its eggs out of water altogether, away from predators, but is then faced with the prospect of continually splashing the fertilized eggs to keep them moist until the hatchlings fall back into the water to grow up.

Everyone knows about the Seahorse where the traditional male/female roles have become reversed. Following fertilization, the eggs are placed in the male's abdominal pouch to develop – surely the fish equivalent of a New Man?

The coldwater Cyprinid, the Bitterling, also has an unusual breeding method and involves using another aquatic creature, the Freshwater Mussel. By means of a long breeding tube, the female Bitterling inserts eggs into the Mussel's mantle out of harm's way; the male's fertilizing sperm is drawn into the mantle as the Mussel takes in water and eggs develop safely inside the bivalve until they are ejected as small fry. This system is to both participant's advantage: the fish fry develop safely and the Mussel ejects its own young which stick to the sides of the Bitterling and get transported elsewhere in the river, thus extending the Mussel's distribution.

All of these spawnings can happen in your aquarium, although to give the fish the best chance of rearing a family (or yourself, if you want a good number of baby fish) it is better to set up a separate breeding aquarium. Here, the 'happy pair' can be brought into breeding condition by being fed the choicest food, any special spawning requirements can be provided – including special precautions to prevent the parent fish from eating their own eggs – and, finally, any baby fish can be raised in safety away from predators that may otherwise threaten them in a community aquarium.

Livebearing fishes include the popular Guppies, Swordtails, Platys and Mollies. In these fishes, the female's eggs are fertilized internally by the male using his specially modified anal fin. The female then incubates the developing eggs inside her body for around a month and then the tiny, miniature fishes are released into the aquarium water ready to swim away into the nearest hiding place.

The majority of the popular livebearing fish species are not found in nature. All the brilliantly coloured varieties seen in the aquatic shops are from captive breeding. Such is the fecundity of livebearing fishes that they offer plenty of potential line-breeding opportunities for you to develop your own new colour strain should you so wish. However, developing any new strain is likely to take years of dedicated care – and lots of new fish tanks to keep the resulting hundreds and thousands of fish in!

Species breeding information

table 12 how different species breed

species	type of breeder	difficulty
Barbs	egg scatterer	easy
Tetras	egg scatterer	easy
Rasboras	mainly egg scatterer	easy
Danios	egg scatterer	easy
Cichlids	egg depositors/ mouthbrooders	easy
Gouramies, Siamese Fighting Fish	bubble-nest builder	easy
Killifish	egg scatterer/egg burier	moderately difficult

species	type of breeder	difficulty
Corydoras catfish	egg depositor	easy
Guppies	livebearer	easy
Swordtails	livebearer	easy
Platys	livebearer	easy
Mollies	livebearer	easy
Goldfish	egg scatterer	easy
Bitterling	egg depositor	moderately difficult
Seahorse	incubator	only for the professionals
Clownfish	egg depositor	becoming more frequent
Neon Goby	egg depositor	becoming more frequent
Cardinal Fish	mouthbrooder	regularly in public aquariums

Breeding fish

Now you know it can be done, it's time to explain how to encourage your fish to breed and how to help them.

We have already seen the best plan is to provide a separate breeding aquarium for the purpose, so let's assume this has been set up with the correct water conditions (if required) and suitable decoration depending on the fish's breeding pattern – bushy plants for egg scatterers and livebearers, rocks and caves for egg depositors and so on.

What to breed? The decision will quite often be taken out of your hands as the fish will breed when they want to, sometimes when you least expect it. But let's assume you want to breed some fish and, whilst you know a little of what's involved, how do you choose the right fish?

Which type of fish is easier to breed, egg-layers or livebearers?

As the first young fish to be seen in any newcomer's tank is likely to be a livebearer, say a Guppy or Platy, some people would advocate beginning with this type of fish. However, as most livebearers are a very willing promiscuous bunch and, as is likely, you've bought several different colour varieties of the same species, you won't be able to guarantee quite what the offspring will look like.

On the other hand, egg-laying fish do breed true, i.e, the youngsters turn out like their parents so the outcome of spawnings are more predictable. But, selecting the parents may be more difficult as adult fish can be hard to sex; then there's the question of getting them to spawn, not always a foregone conclusion even when you have successfully selected a true pair of fish.

As you can see there are advantages and disadvantages of both types of fish so it is a question of personal choice as to which route you take!

Sexing fish

You can't breed fish unless a male and female fish get together. Whilst this is obvious, actually differentiating between the sexes so you can obtain a breeding pair is not always straightforward, especially when there are no visible sexual differences between the fish. In these instances, you have to make an educated guess or seek safety in numbers.

Livebearing fishes are easily sexed. The male fish usually has a modified anal fin although this may not be quite so pronounced in some 'wild' species as in the more popular 'cultivated' species.

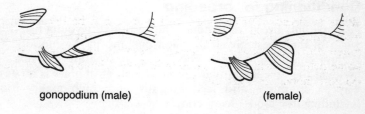

gonopodium (male)　　　　　(female)

figure 29 sexing livebearers

Female livebearers have the usual fan-shaped anal fin and, when developing the young fry within their bodies (they are referred to as being 'gravid' at this stage), appear very distended in the pelvic region.

With egg-laying species, the best guidance is to presume that male fish are generally more brightly coloured, and have more elongated fins and slimmer bodies when viewed from above.

The sexual differences in Angelfish may be seen a little more easily when viewed from the front.

figure 30 sexing Angelfish

Conditioning for breeding

Fish will only breed, or produce the best quality young fish (fry) when in their best physical condition (and in the mood!). To achieve this, it is quite a good idea to separate the sexes – dividing the breeding aquarium with a sheet of glass is an easy way to do this – and feed liberally with high-quality food (including live foods) for a couple of weeks.

Spawning

At the end of this conditioning period, remove the glass partition, or re-unite the fish if previously held in separate tanks and watch the proceedings. Normally, the male fish should chase the female or immediately begin displaying in front of her.

Egg-laying fish chase into bushy plant growths and eggs are expelled, fertilized and land in amongst the plants almost in a twinkling of an eye. Other egglayers may clean a chosen site before laying and fertilizing eggs, or the male fish may, in the case of Siamese Fighting Fish or Gouramies, begin building a bubble-nest under which he hopes to entice the female to expel her eggs.

In some cases, the fertilized eggs may require a period of semi-hydration before they are stimulated into hatching by re-immersion in water. It would not be practicable to use aquatic plants in this context, so artificial spawning mops are used instead, particularly when spawning Killifish. Mops are easily made from wool and a cork and after use can easily be cleaned by washing and then re-used.

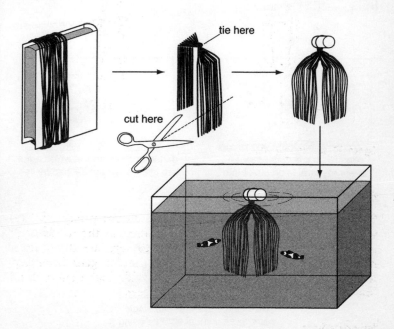

figure 31 making a spawning mop using wool, a book and a cork

Depending on species, Killifish eggs need treating differently if hatching is to be successful. Some eggs hatch within a few days whilst others take not only a lot longer but require a period of semi-hydration first. Keeping the eggs in semi-moist peat moss sealed in a plastic bag for a few weeks is a common practice. Re-immersing the eggs usually triggers hatching and the young fry develop quickly, reflecting the short time they have in nature to grow to adult and spawn themselves before their riverbed dries out again.

It is a good practice to supervise spawnings as not only are you able to watch the proceedings but are on hand to rescue the female should the male fish drive her too hard or even attack her if he feels she is not ready to spawn with him. In your absence, the female will have to seek refuge somewhere in the tank, hence the presence of bushy plants. In most cases, unless the parent fish are of a species that cares for the young or need to be present to look after the fertilized eggs, removing the adult fish immediately spawning has ended will safeguard the eggs from being eaten by them.

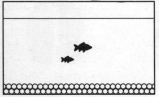

eggs fall in crevices between
layers of marbles on tank base

dense bushy plants in which eggs
are laid not easily reached by fish

fish can be spawned as single
pairs or as a shoal above netting
draped in normally furnished aquarium

figure 32 egg protection strategies

It is possible to shoal-spawn some egglaying species by simply putting together a number of male and female fish after previously conditioning them as described earlier. This is best done by draping a very fine mesh material in the tank and placing all the conditioned adult fish above it; when they spawn, all their eggs fall through the net into the tank and are then beyond reach of the egg-hungry adult fish. The adult fish can then be easily removed in one process by just lifting out the netting material.

Egg protection is not usually necessary with egg-depositing species, bubble-nesters or mouthbrooders as the adult fish will care for the eggs, and subsequent fry, themselves. It is often the case with some egg depositors, especially with young 'first-time spawners,' that the fertilized eggs are eaten by the inexperienced parents.

The solution here is to remove the eggs, on whatever surface they have been laid, to a separate tank and hatch the eggs artificially. A strategically-placed airstone will create a flow of oxygenated water over the eggs and also prevent dirt from settling on them.

After hatching, the eggs remain on the surface of the spawning site absorbing their nutritious yolk-sac for a few days before swimming freely.

When a female livebearer is developing the eggs in her body, her increasing body size gives visual proof of her condition. The gravid female should be placed in a well-planted aquarium in which to deliver her young. Whilst there are plastic breeding traps available to separate the newly born fry from the mother, these tend to be of a small nature and many gravid females find confinement in such traps too stressful and may give birth prematurely.

One of the characteristics of the popular strains of livebearing fish is that females can produce several broods of young from a single mating. This is achieved by her storing sperm in her body, which then fertilizes the next batch of eggs as they become available. Now you can appreciate the problems this may give the fishkeeper when he is trying to isolate, or produce a new colour strain, as ascertaining the parentage of the new fry might not be such an exact science after all!

Raising the young

Once the young fish are free-swimming, all that remains is to give them adequate swimming space and copious amounts of the right size food. One of the best foods for baby fish is Brine Shrimp. You can hatch out Brine Shrimp using salt water to provide a nutritious and disease-free first food for almost any fish fry (see Chapter 12). As the fish grow they can be weaned on to larger live foods such as Grindal- and White-worm and on to crushed flake foods. Bear in mind that extra tank space will be needed, before you embark on a fish-breeding programme.

Breeding case histories

Your first baby fish will probably arrive unannounced, often when you least expect it. You'll be gazing into the tank one day, when suddenly you see something dart past and dash into some aquatic vegetation.

Closer inspection will reveal that it's a tiny fish but you may have to be patient for a few days or weeks more until it grows sufficiently for you to guess what species its parents were!

Usually these chance offspring turn out to be livebearer fry who are much more likely to have survived in the community tank than any egg-laying fish's fry who first has to survive the egg-hatching stage somewhere in the aquarium.

However, should you decide to breed fish deliberately rather than wait for a chance moment to occur, then the following case histories may help you along the road to success.

Platys, Swordtails, Mollies and Guppies

These four popular livebearing fishes pose only one problem when it comes to breeding – where are you going to put all the baby fish? Bear in mind that the record for a Swordtail is around 300 fish, and this could be repeated within a month without the female having recourse to a male Swordtail either, then you can visualize just what could happen once you start breeding fish. But let's follow the course of events.

By now you will have become very familiar with the male livebearer's constant chasing and showing off to the female of his choice (or any other female member of his species that just happens to be passing! You have to be very observant and almost in the right place at the right time to see the actual moment when fertilization occurs, it's that quick.

Soon, the female fish begins to show the effect of the male's brief visitation; her belly begins to swell and often a dark area appears just around the area of her vent. In some cases, the skin of her body becomes stretched so thinly by the number of young fish developing inside her that you can actually see their eyes showing through.

Like all ladies in a 'certain condition' life can become stressful for the female, who may still be pestered by the attentions of male fish. Hopefully, it may be that the aquarium has sufficient aquatic plant life for her to be able to hide away for some respite and this same plant covering may well act as a sanctuary for any young fry once they emerge from their mother's body.

The female delivers the young fish after about 30 days. Naturally you will want to save as many of them as possible from being instant food for the other fish in the aquarium – or even their own parents. How to do this can be solved in two ways. One method is to place the female (now referred to as being gravid, rather than 'pregnant') in a small confining tank floated inside a bigger tank. Her tank has small slots in it so that the young fish can swim out into the larger water space and escape any tendency she may have to eat them. This is fine in theory but in practice things can go wrong, especially if you move the female into these small quarters at the wrong time, i.e. too near to the end of her 'confinement' period.

Stress of the move may well cause her to abort the youngsters prematurely and they will not survive. There is no point either in floating the 'breeding trap' tank, as it is called, in the community aquarium itself for all that will happen, even if the female goes to full term, is that all the other fish will queue up under the trap for a continuous supply of live food.

As you need a separate tank to use the breeding trap correctly, the best plan would be to use this smaller tank as a nursery tank. Don't forget, you've hopefully still got that quarantine/hospital tank somewhere that would do admirably. As mentioned earlier, the quarantine/hospital tank need not be spacious, anything above 25 cm (10") long will suffice.

The best scenario for our expectant lady will be in a well-planted tank. The 'well-planted' description does not necessarily mean artistically planted as might be the case in the main aquarium. All that is needed is enough shelter for the baby fish, there will be no hiding places required for mum as she will be the only adult fish in the tank. A certain number of tall plants around the tank in clumps together with some bushy types and a good covering of a floating species (*Riccia* is fine) or Indian Fern, *Ceratopteris thalictroides*, with its tangle of roots tangling down into the water will give the youngsters the safety areas they require.

You should keep an eye on the female to check that she is progressing well; you can transfer her into the 'delivery tank' as soon as you see that she is gravid – the earlier the better.

You will know when she has delivered her young as she will lose her fatness in the belly region. Now, it is up to you to decide how long you will leave her to recuperate in the quiet nursery tank before returning her to the main aquarium. Of course, you won't want her seeking out her offspring so feed her in the usual way. Should she take an interest in looking for the baby fish then you have no alternative but to return her to the main aquarium.

Livebearer fry are more capable than most new fishkeepers realize. There is no need to feed them microscopic particles of food; they will attack flake food quite voraciously, although crumbling up the larger flakes might help them out a little.

'Fry food' and 'growth food' are usually higher in protein than the normal flake food and are specifically formulated for the feeding of young fish. You should supplement this with live food if at all possible. Newly-hatched Brine Shrimp is excellent, as is the use of Grindal-worm and White-worm and you can find details of culturing these first foods in Chapter 12.

From now on, it's a case of growing on the young fish. Frequent partial water changes will help keep them healthy, active and growing. Splitting up the numbers may be necessary if the nursery tank becomes too small (or you want to use it for another purpose). Some quality control may need to be done with any weak or malformed fish being discarded; you may, if so inclined, or if the colour strain of the fish is to be preserved (or improved), segregate those of suitable colouration for future breeding, isolating them from any colour strain which would otherwise weaken the quality of the strain you are trying to develop.

For those fascinated by permutations, the Mendelian Laws of Heredity can make interesting reading. To give but a taste:

breeding a female Guppy of wild colouration with a male Gold Guppy will produce a first generation of Guppies all with wild colouration because of the dominance of the wild colouration gene. However, moving on to breed between these offspring the results for the next generation will be 25 per cent wild colouration (pure), 50 per cent wild-type colouration (through dominance) and 25 per cent Gold (pure).

You can see that attempting to produce a 'new' colour strain is not just a case of blue and yellow will equal green but probably all the shades in between. Add to this the extra complications that arise should you also wish to develop, say, finnage refinements and body shape modifications as well as colour then you're in for a very long haul. Time to reach for the calculator and order all those extra tanks!

Zebra Danios

Many fishkeepers sometimes get a little embarrassed when they admit that their first fish breeding was a livebearer, feeling that they, as fishkeepers, didn't have very much to do with the event. Whilst this may be true to a certain extent, it nevertheless does mean that the fish had been kept in correct conditions and were sufficiently healthy to want to reproduce and this must be a reflection of their owner's skill in maintaining the aquarium over a period of time.

However, with an egg-laying species, the aquarist can have a great deal of control over what fish he wants to breed and, just as importantly, when.

It should be said here, that fish will breed whenever they choose inasmuch that should a ripe male and female encounter each other then they will probably spawn spontaneously in the aquarium anyway. Without the care and attention of the fishkeeper, the eggs from egg-scattering species especially will more likely than not be eaten by the other fish in the tank and no fry will be seen. The fry from egg-depositing fish stand a better chance as first of all their parents will prepare and defend a spawning site prior to spawning and also guard any subsequent fry afterwards. Let's suppose you want to try your hand at breeding something deliberately, and have taken the advice of many experienced fishkeepers by choosing that popular Cyprinid, the Zebra Danio.

First of all, we must ensure that the fish are 'in the mood' to breed rather than just put a male and female together and hope for the best. 'Absence makes the heart grow fonder' is one way of putting it but, realistically, separating the would-be parents is based on a practical rather than emotional supposition.

It is possible that should you simply select a male and female and put them together to spawn then one of them might just have spawned without your knowledge; in which case, the attempt to spawn them would be fruitless.

By separating the sexes prior to spawning, you can ensure that they are in the best condition; feeding them copious amounts of quality food (including live food) will make the female fill with eggs. This conditioning process can take a couple of weeks or so. The best way to do it might be to put the female into the breeding tank first before introducing the well-fed male later.

Sexing the fish is fairly straightforward: the male fish is more slender than the female and if you look at a female, even when she is not full of eggs, there is a definite kink in the horizontal stripes along the body just to the rear of the dorsal fin.

Like all Cyprinids, the Zebra Danio is no respector of new-laid eggs, including its own. As described earlier, there are several ways to prevent egg eating. Any method that separates the adult fish from reaching their newly-laid eggs is acceptable.

One popular method is to cover the bottom of the aquarium with a layer or two of glass marbles (the eggs fall between the marbles beyond the reach of the adults). Alternatively you can use a bunch or two of dense plants in the spawning area: as the male chases the female into the plants, she releases the eggs which after fertilization fall into the dense plants away from the attentions of the adults.

There is no reason why you cannot 'flock spawn' fish. If you have several Zebra Danios then separating all the females from all the males during the conditioning period should give you more Zebra Danio fry than you'd believe possible upon the adults' reunion! But there's still the problem of egg protection.

The answer is to drape a piece of fine netting across the entire water surface area of the spawning tank so that it hangs a few centimetres below the surface; weight the corners down with small pebbles. Now all that is needed is to introduce all the pre-conditioned fish (both sexes) into the water above the net.

When the males chase the females, any eggs that are released and fertilized then fall through the net into the tank beneath before the adults have time to realize what's going on. The eggs are safe! In order to return the adult fish to their previous aquarium all you do is lift out the net (take the pebbles out first!). The fish are caught all at once with no stress at all.

Meanwhile, the fertilized eggs are quietly hatching and in a few days you will see what looks like tiny splinters of glass hanging on the sides of the aquarium. These are your new Zebra Danios.

Because they are not exactly sizeable fry, they will require quite small particle-sized food at first. There are preparations of liquid fry food available at your aquatic store and it's a simple task to add a few drops of this at the recommended times to their tank. It may help if you keep a low-level light burning over their tank so that they can feed 24 hours a day.

It is important during these first few days not to over-feed – a difficult task, as you'll never be exactly sure how many baby mouths you've got to feed. Therefore, regular partial water changes are of the highest importance, if water conditions in the nursery tank are not to be compromised.

As the fry grow, then the feeding routine can mirror that outlined earlier for livebearers, with a gradual progression on to larger particle foods. Again, spacing out of fry into larger tanks may be necessary.

Angelfish

(Colour Plate 11.) So far, the fish we have examined have shown no apparent responsibility for the care of their fry – indeed, the every opposite may be true. However, with Cichlids, the picture changes completely.

Here we have a species that chooses its mate, jointly selects and defends a spawning site, spawns out in the open and then safeguards its young offspring against all-comers. Can you imagine what it's like to witness such a sequence?

Although Angelfish will spawn in the community aquarium (much to the discomfort of the other fishes), it is far better to give them a tank of their own where they can become parents without the added stress of having to consider the presence of other fishes.

If possible, the Angelfish spawning tank should have a fair depth of water, 38 cm (15") or so. It should be furnished with some broad-leaved plants, such as Amazon Swordplants and a few pieces of slate (possible spawning sites) leaning against the sides of the aquarium; these pieces of slate should be fairly long and can be nearly vertical.

A good trigger to set Angelfish spawning is a slight rise in temperature, so set the thermostat to a couple of degrees higher than in the main aquarium.

To obtain a compatible pair of Angelfish – they seem to like to choose their own mates – the best way is to buy half a dozen young Angelfish, grow them up and let them self-select. There are numerous strains of Angelfish around and should you have a mixed selection then don't be surprised if say, a Silver strain pairs off with a Gold strain, they're not that selective. If you want to minimize peculiar coloured offspring then it might be best to stick with one particular strain.

So, one day you notice that in your community tank two Angelfish are going around together, perhaps shooing away the other fish from one particular area. This may be the early signs of selecting a spawning site. Look closely at the vent areas of the Angelfish and you will probably be able to see the white ovipositor tube projecting from the vent. This tube is through which the female extrudes eggs and the male his sperm. Sexing Angelfish can be a hit and miss affair and although many authorities have decreed certain clues, there is only one definite clue to decide things for you.

The size and shape of the male's ovipositor is different to that of the female. The male's ovipositor is not so broad and it rather pointed; the female's ovipositor has to be thicker in order to pass the eggs through it whereas that of the male only has to pass liquid sperm. Conjecture about the sexes of the fish may be the subject of some discussion, but really it is only relevant at spawning time – when the fish have already made their minds up about things – and this is the only time you will be able to see their ovipositors anyway. Now is the time to give them their own quarters.

Angelfish spend a few days selecting a spawning site, which may be a leaf surface, a piece of slate, a filter tube or even the front glass! Whatever they choose, they will then clean it scrupulously by biting off any debris and spitting it out.

When satisfied that all is well, the female fish will then make a few practice passes up the spawning site, pressing her ventral surface against its whole length, with her long bony pelvic fins folded back along her body.

Eventually, she will repeat this exercise but this time eggs will be laid on the surface of the spawning site. The male will have been watching all these manoeuvres and soon will make similar passes up the spawning site to fertilize the eggs.

Keeping the fertilized eggs clean, and supplied with a flow of oxygenated water, becomes the most important task for the two adult Angelfish. They will fan the eggs continuously with their pectoral fins and, without warning, are likely to transfer the whole batch of eggs to a new, previously selected and cleaned site, much to your consternation as you may have thought they were eating them!

After a couple of days, the eggs hatch and become a wriggling mass of tails and egg yolks. The fry will remain on the spawning site for about a week before they rise, as one, and become free-swimming young fish. During this time the parents continually take them into their mouths to clean them before returning them to the spawning site surface; you have to be brave to watch this – there's an overwhelming urge to net out the parents to protect the fry!

Now the parents really begin to worry! They actually herd the young to where they want them to be; any fry that ventures too far from the crowd is rapidly sought out, taken into the parent's mouth and spat back with his brothers and sisters. The parents even put the flock of fry to bed each night, back on the spawning site.

Feeding the young should commence with newly-hatched Brine Shrimp. Feed the parents their normal flake food as normal; any flakes that settle on the tank base may be fanned up by the parents, taken in and spat out as miniaturized food for their young.

But suppose the adult fish do not conform to this expected parental role, but decide to neglect or start to eat the eggs? What can you do then? You must remove the parents obviously and put them back into the main aquarium. You then have to take over as guardian of the fry.

Place an airstone near to the spawning site so as to create a flow of water over the eggs. Carry out partial water changes every other day in the fry tank to minimize fungal growth on the eggs. Cleanliness is the most important factor in artificially raising eggs away from the natural parents.

Do not add liquid fry food to the tank until the fry are free-swimming and actively looking for food. To do so, would be to waste the food and also run the risk of polluting the tank; remember, during the first seven days the fry are absorbing nourishment from their yolk-sacs and have no need of extra food.

The same previously made comments about feeding and leaving the light on over the tank 24 hours a day applies to these fry too.

After a couple of weeks of regular feeding with Brine Shrimp and so on should result in the tiny fry taking on the high dorsal and long anal fin typical of the Angelfish and you know that you have successfully bred another species.

Dwarf Cichlids

Staying with Cichlids, can you imagine how frustrating it can be to know you have a pair of these clever fish spawning but you can never get around to actually seeing them do it? Such is often the case with Dwarf Cichlids who are quite secretive spawners. Many spawn in rocky caves, often upside down on the ceiling, just to be different.

The Kribensis, *Pelvicachromis pulcher*, is a modest-sized Cichlid from West Africa. The male has a spade-shaped caudal fin whilst the female's main claim to fame is her purple colouration which intensifies at breeding time.

These fish will certainly spawn in the community aquarium and are stout defenders of both their spawning site and subsequent fry. It is not unusual for them to 'disappear' for a disconcerting period of time only to eventually reappear with a couple of dozen youngsters in tow. However it is obviously best to set up a separate breeding tank for them.

Again a planted tank is recommended with the added furnishing of a flowerpot laid on its side on the substrate. You should enlarge the drainage hole in the bottom to allow the fish to enter and exit the pot from that end should they prefer to. Alternatively, short pieces of plastic pipe may also make potential spawning sites.

As with other Cichlids, a pair of Kribensis will normally pair off spontaneously should you have a number of them grown up from young in your collection. You could also buy a pair from your dealer, using the sex identification guide previously mentioned, but there is no guarantee that they will turn into a compatible pair bent on producing a family for you.

Once decided on a lady of his choice, the male fish will display in front of her with many turnings and U-shape bendings of his body. At this time too, his colours will be intensified.

They will disappear into the flowerpot or pipe to clean a spawning site on which eggs are laid by the female and fertilized by the male.

When the fry emerge from their hatching period and are free-swimming, the female's colours again intensify possibly to facilitate fry–adult communication. Her belly turns a deep rich purple whilst her fins take on a sooty black appearance, especially the pelvic fins which she continually flicks as if signalling to the fry.

Again, the parents will herd the young and protect them against any possible threat.

Raising the fry to young fish follows the normal feeding patterns described earlier and the fry grow quickly.

It is often the case that there is a predominance of one sex or another in the brood of youngsters. Reports suggest that this state of affairs can be altered (perhaps producing too many of the other sex next time?) by tinkering with the water chemistry, i.e., raising or lowering the pH from what is was before. Caution must be exercised when altering the water chemistry; at the very least you might put off the parents' willingness to breed – even though you wouldn't be able to see them doing it.

Dwarf Gourami

(Colour Plate 19.) Cichlids are not the only species to create a spawning site or to practise parental control over their young. Members of the Labyrinthfish group, such as Gouramies and Siamese Fighting Fish – also have a refined method of reproduction

Again, it is preferable to give these fish a separate tank in which to spawn; this is not just out of courtesy but perhaps to preserve the tranquillity of the community aquarium. In this example, the Dwarf Gourami, *Colisa lalia*, might be thought a peaceful species but during the build up to spawning the male turns quite ferocious. In a tank containing mostly livebearers, one ardent Dwarf Gourami managed to kill off the majority of the other species before anyone realized what was happening.

There is no difficulty in sexing these fish. The male's flanks are adorned with bright red diagonal stripes and as the onset of spawning occurs his throat and chest region take on a turquoise hue. In contrast, the female can de said to be a little dowdy, just a slivery blue-grey colour with only a hint of lines on her side. Of course, following a period of conditioning she will fill out as the eggs build up in her body.

The procedure of the spawning ritual is this: the male constructs a floating bubble-nest using saliva and also fragments of plant material. Usually this is placed in a quiet area of the tank, away from any flow of water returning from the filtration system. The nest extends 2–3 cm (1") into the air and has a diameter of around 10 cm (4"). At the end of this construction phase, the male then entices the female to inspect the structure and, if approval appears forthcoming then the next part of the spawning occurs. However, should the male decide that the female is not quite acceptable to him or she disdains his invitation and shows little interest in his labours then it is likely that he will attack her.

It is therefore important that the spawning tank is well-planted so that the female can escape from the male until she can be rescued (by removal from the tank by the fishkeeper). Of course, plant material is also welcomed by the male to provide building materials for the bubble-nest.

It is possible to condition a pair of Dwarf Gouramies in the spawning tank by using a piece of glass or sheet plastic to divide the tank into two sections. Simply place each fish in their respective halves of the tank and feed well for a couple of weeks.

At the end of the conditioning period, remove the partition and watch what happens, being prepared all the time to step in if the female is attacked. It may be that if a sheet of glass had been used as a partition, the male fish will have had continuous sightings of the female during the conditioning period and may well have begun, or even completed, building a bubble-nest in anticipation of their reunion.

Assuming that all goes to plan, the two fish will embrace beneath the nest, the female will roll over on to her back and the released eggs will be fertilized by the male and float up into the bubble-nest. At the end of the spawning action, the female will probably make a dash into the nearest plants, at which time she should be removed as she will take no further part in the spawning procedure.

Left to his own devices, the male sets about patrolling beneath the nest, regularly repairing parts of it that may be disintegrating and restoring any of the fry that fall out.

One problem with the Dwarf Gourami is the size of the fry or, to be more specific, their need for tiny food. Here the fishkeeper must fall back on to liquid fry food at least, or try a piece of hard-boiled egg yolk squeezed in a piece of cloth in some aquarium water. Do not add too much for fear of tank water pollution. Another possibility is to use 'green water'. This is something that is anathema to pond owners but it can contain microscopic life forms that the fry can eat. Unfortunately, this must obviously be produced ahead of the spawning in order to be ready when needed, so it takes a little forethought to prepare a jar of water and stand it in bright sunshine for a couple for weeks, although you could time it to coincide with the parents' conditioning period.

Eventually the fry will reach a size where they can move on to the usual fry-feeding programme.

There is often quite a high mortality rate of the fry. Some say this occurs around the second week and often point it to cold air entering the aquarium when the hood is opened. To this end, many drape a towel over the hood to exclude draughts but this must be done with caution if the hood is not to over-heat from the lights inside.

troubleshooting

In this chapter you will learn:
- dealing with power failures and leaks
- equipment problems
- overcoming algae growth.

This chapter deals with a small selection of aquarium-related (not fish-related) problems that either crop up from time to time or that people worry about in advance of the event happening.

Power failure

What do you do if there is a power cut? Don't panic. The aquarium will lose heat very slowly and probably will not have reached a dangerously low temperature by the time the power is restored. Wrapping the tank in bubble-wrap or old newspapers will conserve the tank's warmth if the power cut looks set to continue for a long time. In extreme cases, you could heat up bottles of water (using any alternative heating method) and stand them in the tank.

In summer, should the tank over-heat (it has been known!), floating a sealed bag of ice cubes in the tank will bring down the temperature but, equally important at this time, is to add extra aeration as an increase in water temperature means a decrease in oxygen available in the water.

Leaks

It is not unknown for a set-up aquarium to spring a leak but, unless there is a large visible crack across a glass panel, there is often no need to imagine that a flooded carpet is imminent. If the tank is new, the leak will often seal itself as microscopic dirt finds its way into the leak, so give it a little time to sort itself out before taking more drastic action.

Should a leak be pinpointed to a weakened seam in the tank, then follow the procedure outlined in Chapter 09.

Of course, a pool of water, or a damp patch, on the floor next to the aquarium might not be from the tank itself but from an external piece of equipment. Check that all hoses connecting external filters and isolating taps are securely tightened. Perhaps a sealing ring in the filter body is not seated correctly? Sometimes a hood not quite replaced exactly can leak condensation drips.

Filters

A filter may stop for three basic reasons – a clogged medium, a clogged impeller or an airlock.

Regular maintenance will soon prevent the first two causes from occurring. It is obvious that the medium will clog over a period of time but the impeller is also likely to be affected by deposits of slime that build up around it. Don't overlook this vital part of the filter when servicing.

Dislodging an airlock, usually found in external filters, may be as simple as shaking the filter body gently, but in some cases you may have to invert it to dislodge that stubborn bubble of air.

Air-pumps

A sudden loss of air, usually accompanied by a loud buzzing noise, indicates that the rubber diaphragm inside the air-pump is split and no longer capable of 'pumping'.

A general falling off in performance points to a blocked air-valve in the final air-chamber part of the pump or a badly clogged air-filter on the pump's input.

Before attempting any repairs, always switch off the power. Replacing the diaphragm is fairly straightforward but greater care (and perhaps some dexterity) is required to replace the tiny air-valves. The air-filter is a piece of felt material inserted in the base of the air-pump – and it's an important part of the pump that many fishkeepers overlook.

If you use an air-pump to supply several devices in the aquarium – filters, airstones, etc. – and one of them fails, then the cause of the problem may be a clogged air-control valve in the airline rather than a fault with the pump itself.

Airstones too have a habit of blocking due to build-up of minerals, more so in the marine aquarium. Where airstones are made of sintered glass, boiling them may unclog them but those made of beechwood are best discarded and simply replaced.

Algae

Probably the most common problem in the aquarium, whether it's newly set up or well established, is that of green algae growing everywhere.

Algae thrives on nutrients in the water and on excessive light. Cut down on the supply of these factors and the green troubles will fade away.

Nutrients in the water are generally due to over-feeding, rather than to high levels of nitrate already in the water supply. Any uneaten food simply adds to the nitrate in the water.

There may not be an excess of light at all: it may be that there are not enough aquatic plants to make use of all the light energy available. Algae can be out-competed for nutrients by planting more plants. There is no harm in experimenting with different durations of lighting, but bear in mind that most aquarium plants need 12 hours of light each day. Varying the light intensity is more difficult these days with fluorescent lighting as, unless the tank is lit by several tubes, in which case you might turn off a tube for a period, shading is the only way of controlling the intensity.

We have already mentioned using 'natural defences' against algae in the form of algae-eating fishes, both in freshwater and marine aquariums.

Fish behaviour

Apart from odd fish behaviour due to illness or poor tank conditions, occasionally you will get a fish that doesn't want to fit in or develops anti-social behaviour some months after its introduction.

This can be accounted for by two or three things. The fish may be showing an incompatibility characteristic that you should have uncovered before you bought the fish, for example it may need to be kept in a shoal. More likely though is that the fish has become an adult and is simply exercising its natural tendencies with respect to claiming territory, or protecting its own, especially when assuming breeding condition.

In terms of remedies, a bullying fish could be returned to the shop, a lonely fish might perk up when more of its own species are added. Alternatively, you could always set up another aquarium for the benefit of that would-be breeder.

7 the Show must go on

In this chapter you will learn:
- all about fish Shows
- expanding your fish keeping interests
- where to get help

Each year, on most weekend days from March to November, there'll be thousands of fish on the move around the country. They'll have been taken out of their home aquariums, loaded into insulated boxes, driven hundreds of miles to some village hall and then exhibited in small, bare tanks, simply to be told how good or bad they are. The rewards are slight, save for the pleasure of owning a prize-winning specimen for, unlike some other animal shows, there are no pedigrees involved in fishkeeping – so no lucrative stud fees for that super Guppy!

Aquarium Open Shows are normally one-day affairs, with only the larger national exhibitions extending perhaps over a weekend. As in dog and cat shows, fishes are generally divided into breeds or classes, which are then judged; there may, for example, be Classes for Barbs, Characins, Cichlids, Anabantids, Killifishes, Catfishes or Livebearers. Other Classes will be for pairs of fishes (male and female shown together), 'breeder's team' (four or six fish from a single spawning,) furnished aquaria, terrariums and aquatic plants.

How can you possibly judge one fish, say, a Guppy against a Discus? All Shows use a pointing system that covers a fish's five main characteristics – size, body, colour, fins, condition and deportment, and each of these categories may be allocated a set number of points, usually totalling 100.

Aquarium Societies will also hold Table or Bowl Shows at their evening meetings, and these may be broadened out to include neighbouring Societies on an inter-Society championship basis. There are also specialist Societies' Shows, which are restricted to certain families or groups of fishes – Siamese Fighting Fishes, Discus, Catfishes, Fancy Goldfishes, Livebearers.

Many arguments rage over the merits or otherwise of aquarium Shows; many decry the competitive aspect of the hobby for the 'trophy-hunting' effect it has on some people, who must win at all costs.

Strict codes of practice exist to ensure that fish are exhibited under the best conditions, tanks have to be of a minimum size (even a 2 cm fish must have a 10 cm tank), larger tanks may have filtration systems fitted and a treatment area must be allocated, so that any fish that may fall sick during the show is promptly cared for.

Nevertheless, the aquarium Show has several good points: here you can see a large collection of adult fishes in prime condition (especially new species) amid artistically furnished aquarium settings; Shows provide a meeting place for experts and beginners alike, an ideal opportunity to exchange ideas and information. The exhibition of fishes provides one of the biggest stimuli to the continuation of the hobby.

taking it further

The good news is that you're not alone, nor are you very far away from a helping hand. Sources of help, should the need arise, include:

• The aquatic dealer.
• The local aquarium society.
• Monthly hobby magazines.
• Aquatic manufacturers.
• The Internet.
• The local library.

Obviously with any problems arising with equipment or fish purchased, your immediate course of action is to ask for guidance from the aquatic dealer. Your relationship with the dealer is important and much can be resolved if he knows about your purchases and aquarium set-up. Always provide as much information as possible. The dealer will want to know:

• The size of tank.
• How many and what types of fish are in it.
• Your feeding regime.
• Your filtration system and water quality details.
• Fish behaviour (plus symptoms, in event of disease).
• What new things you might have introduced recently.
• What action you've already taken.

A good supporting hand can be found at your local aquarium society, if there is one. Picking the collective brains of people already keeping fish in your area is bound to uncover with the answer to your problem. You should be able to find out the whereabouts of such societies in your area from the town hall amenities officer or the national fishkeeping organization.

Monthly hobby magazines cover the whole range of fishkeeping interests at all levels of proficiency. Most have 'readers' problems' pages in which residents experts offer advice on a wide range of problems.

All aquatic manufacturers offer advisory services not only for their own products but also will try to answer any fishkeeping queries.

The Internet has to be the largest storehouse of easily accessible knowledge in the world and for those with Internet access there should be no difficulty in finding answers to problems, researching new fish, checking on breeding techniques or even finding out the latest scientific names. All is possible at the click of the mouse.

Finally, books such as this still remain a favourite source of information. You can't always take the computer screen up to the aquarium to compare pictures or notes but you can with a book. All libraries have good pet sections and some may even allow you to photocopy relevant details if you don't want to take the book away.

Addresses

Federation of British Aquatic Societies
44 Weeks Road
Ryde
Isle of Wight PO33 2TL
http://www.fbas.co.uk/

Periodicals

Practical Fishkeeping
Bretton Court
Bretton
Peterborough
Cambridgeshire PE3 8DZ
http://www.practicalfishkeeping.co.uk/

Tropical Fish
Freestyle Publications Ltd
Alexander House
Ling Road
Tower Park
Poole
Dorset BH12 4NZ

Tropical World
Dukinfield Publications Ltd
PO Box 101
Plymouth PL7 2XY
http://www.tropicalworldmagazine.com/

Marine World
Aero Mill
Church
Accrington
Lancashire BB5 4JS
http://www.marineworldmagazine.com/

Further reading

David Alderton *Encyclopedia of Aquarium & Pond Fish*, Dorling Kindersley (2005).

Vincent B. Hargreaves *The Complete Book of the Marine Aquarium*, Interpet Publishing (2002).

Dick Mills *Aquarist's Encyclopedia*, Blandford Press (1983).

Dick Mills *Keeping Goldfish*, Blandford Press (1985).

Dick Mills *You and Your Aquarium*, Dorling Kindersley (1986).

Dick Mills *Aquarium Fishes*, Dorling Kindersley (1993).

Dick Mills *Encyclopedia of Aquarium Fish*, Barrons/Quarto (2000).

Dick Mills *500 Ways to be a Better Marine Fishkeeper*, Interpet Publishing (2000).

Dick Mills *Mini Encyclopedia: The Marine Aquarium*, Interpet Publishing (2004).

Dick Mills *The Aquarium Fish Handbook*, Barrons/Quarto (2004).

Geoff Rogers/Nick Fletcher *Focus on Aquarium Fish*, Interpet Publishing (2005).

Gina Sandford *Mini Encyclopedia: The Tropical Aquarium*, Interpet Publishing (2004).

The Federation of British Aquatic Societies

Formed in 1938, the Federation of British Aquatic Societies (FBAS) continues to pursue its primary aims of supporting and promoting the interests of its member Societies and to also maintain links with similar organizations at home and abroad.

Following the publication of the first aquatic hobby magazine *The Amateur Aquarist* in 1924 (to become the renowned *The Aquarist & Pondkeeper* over the coming 80 years), interest in fishkeeping surged only to be set back, understandably, by the Second World War.

In 1947, the FBAS published its first set of 'Standards' for exhibiting fish and, from then on, gradually established itself as the largest aquatic governing body in the United Kingdom.

Over two dozen informative booklets were produced over the subsequent 30 years with the emphasis being on descriptions of fish species, particularly in context with exhibiting. These booklets with their accurate line drawings were supplemented by the annually-updated booklet containing fish sizes of those species most likely to be kept in captivity. As 20 per cent of any points awarded to an exhibited fish were in regard to its overall physical size, this booklet was eagerly awaited each year, as exhibitors sought to see what 'amendments' had been made to previous editions and also what new species had been included.

A *Programme Aids Booklet* was produced annually that outlined public places of aquatic interest (public aquariums, water gardens, museums etc.), together with audio visual programmes produced by the FBAS and lists of people willing to judge at fish Shows or give lectures to Societies. In addition to this information, the *Yearbook*, as it became known, also contained contact details of all the Federation Officers and Show Trophies available.

Currently, the Federation is very much involved with considering the implications of governmental legislation in the light of the proposed Animal Welfare Bill especially in how it will affect the continuance of its member Societies' activities.

Throughout the 1960s and 1970s it was usual for several major aquatic Shows to be held around the country. Sponsored by the various hobby magazines these events at London's Alexandra Palace and Royal Horticultural Hall were very popular.

With the introduction of the Internet, it became clear that there was no need in trying to compete with the flood of aquatic information (if you'll pardon the play on words) now available and the Federation turned its attention to maintaining its Society base, addressing the problem of attracting new members.

To do this, it mounted information stands at the Hampton Court Palace Flower Show for many years; similarly, the Chelsea Flower Show and also the National Amateur Garden Show at Shepton Mallett were also supported.

A current popular FBAS-organized activity is the annual Supreme Festival of Fishkeeping. This event is a whole weekend of fishkeeping, embracing all aspects of the hobby. Naturally there are competitive exhibitions for Goldfish, Koi and Tropical species but these are enhanced by the presence of trade displays, guest lecturers and, of course, a highly enjoyable social scene.

Recently, with the advent of computer technology, the Federation has moved on to produce its own video programmes. These may be video versions of illustrated lectures or of live aquatic events. All of these programmes may be hired by member Societies (on VHS tapes) or purchased on DVD format by individuals.

The FBAS now operates its own website:
(http://www.fbas. co.uk) which features a wealth of information, especially in the care of fish in captivity, whether in the home aquarium, pond or whilst at exhibitions.

glossary

Acidic Water having a pH value of less than 7.

Activated charcoal Special charcoal used as a filter medium to adsorb dissolved substances from the aquarium water.

Adipose (fin) Small extra fin between the dorsal fin and the caudal fin.

Aeration The movement of water (to aid gaseous exchanges) created by the introduction of a supply of compressed air into the aquarium.

Aerobic Requiring, dependent upon, oxygen.

Air-pump Source of compressed air, usually a diaphragm driven by a small electric vibrator system.

Airstone (aerator, diffuser) A porous block of wood or sintered glass through which air is passed to emerge as a stream of small bubbles.

Air-tubing (airline) Neoprene tubing connecting an air-pump to the airstone or filter.

Algae Tiny, unicellular plants which may coat the entire aquarium or cause a green cloudiness in the water.

Alkaline Water having a pH value greater than 7.

All-glass (tank) Five pieces of glass glued together to form a container without incorporating a frame.

Anabantid Fish having an auxiliary breathing organ in the head (Gouramies, Siamese Fighting Fish).

Anaerobic Not requiring, independent of, oxygen.

Anal (fin) Single fin underneath the fish similar to a ship's keel.

Annual fishes Fishes living in streams which dry up completely each year, such as Killifishes.

Aquarium Watertight container in which fishes live; also the complete furnished tank.

Aquascape The underwater scene; in Britain, another name for a combined aquarium/terrarium furnished with plants and other features above the waterline.

Artemia salina See **Brine Shrimp**.

Barb (family) Small, deep-bodied fishes of the genus *Barbus*, which originate from India, the Far East and elsewhere.

Barbels Group of whisker-like growths around the mouth of, for example, Barbs and Catfishes.

Biological filter See **Undergravel filter**.

Brackish water Water containing a measure of salt, but not as saline as seawater.

Breeding trap Small compartment in which a gravid livebearer female can give birth, designed so that the mother fish cannot eat the young; it may cause premature birth by upsetting the mother-to-be.

Brine Shrimp (*Artemia salina*) Shrimp found in salt lakes whose eggs may be stored dry over long periods. When hatched they provide a nutritious, disease-free food ideal for fish fry.

Cable Tidy Connecting junction box for electrical wiring terminations. Has switches for lighting and the air-pump.

Catfishes Bottom-dwelling fishes, quite recognizable by their well-developed barbels.

Caudal (fin) The tail, or single fin at the rear end of a fish.

Caudal peduncle Narrow part of the fish's body which connects to the caudal fin.

Characins Large group of freshwater fishes which contains such diverse fishes as the Piranha and the Neon Tetra.

Cichlids Perch-like freshwater fishes, which exercise parental care; includes the Angelfish and Discus.

Coldwater fishes Fishes needing no heating of their water.

Conditioning The bringing of fishes into prime state of health, either for exhibiting or breeding.

Cover glass Sheet of glass placed above the tank, but below the light fittings; reduces evaporation and prevents fish escaping.

Crown (of plant) Junction between plant stem and root.

Cuttings Pieces of aquatic plants consisting of a severed leaf or stem and used for propagation.

Daphnia (*D. pulex*) The Water Flea, a freshwater crustacean used as a live food.

Dorsal Pertaining to the fish's back.

Dorsal (fin) Single fin on the top of the fish's body. Some species have two.

Egglayers Fishes that lay eggs which are fertilized and hatched outside the female's body.

Family Group containing genera (see **Genus**).

Fancy Goldfish Any of the cultivated varieties of the Common Goldfish.

Fertile Describes sexually mature fish, or eggs containing developing fish embryos.

Filter Device for cleansing the aquarium water by mechanical or biological means. May be situated either inside or outside the aquarium and be air- or electrically-powered.

Filter medium Any material used as a trapping device in a filter system.

Fin Propelling and steering organs of a fish, usually seven in number; dorsal, anal, caudal, adipose (if present), pectoral (two), and pelvic or ventral (two).

Fin Rot Disease in which the tissue between the fin rays degenerates.

Foam-fractionation See **Protein skimmer**.

Fry The young of a fish.

Fungus A cotton-wool-like growth caused by bacteria on the body of the fish.

Gallon Measure of liquid capacity: 1 Imperial gallon = 1.2 US gallons = 4.55 litres; 1 US gallon = 0.83 Imp. gallons = 3.7 litres. 1 Imp. gallon of freshwater weighs 10 Ib (45 kgs); I US gallon weighs 8.3 Ib (3.76 kg).

Genus A group sharing common characteristics usually containing several species.

Gills Organs by which the fish breathes.

Gonopodium The male livebearing fish's copulatory organ.

Gravel tidy Mesh material placed horizontally in the substrate to prevent fish from digging too deeply.

Gravid Pregnant; a term used for livebearer females.

Guanin Crystals of urea deposited beneath the skin which produces iridescences.

Handstripping See **Stripping**.

Hard (water) Water containing an abundance of dissolved minerals.

Hardness (of water) Measurement of the amount of dissolved salts in water.

Heater Glass-encased electric element acting as an immersion heater to warm the aquarium water.

Hood Tank lid housing the lighting equipment, often acting as a reflector as well as a protective cover.

Infertile Not able to reproduce; often applied to fish eggs which do not produce young.

Infusoria Minute organisms which can be used as food for fry; may be cultured (infused) by the fishkeeper.

Killifishes Members of the *Cyprinodontidae* family which inhabit streams that may dry up every year; they are often known as 'annual fishes'. The name comes from *killi*, a Dutch word for ditch.

Labyrinthfishes Members of the *Anabantidae* family, having a labyrinthine accessory breathing organ in the head.

Labyrinth organ Accessory breathing organ allowing some fishes to breathe air directly from the atmosphere.

Lateral line A vibration-sensing system appearing as a row of tiny holes along the sides of the fish.

Length Total body length; caudal fin is not included.

Litre Metric measure of liquid capacity. 1 litre = 0.22 Imperial gallon = 0.26 US gallon.

Livebearers Fishes whose fertile eggs develop inside the body of the female.

Marine Pertaining to sea water.

Milt The fertilizing fluid of the male fish.

Mops Bunches of nylon wool placed in the breeding tank to act as receptacles for eggs in place of plants; widely used by Killifish breeders.

Mouthbreeder (-brooder) Species of fishes which incubate the fertile eggs in the mouth of the female fish.

Nauplius The newly-hatched stage of the Brine Shrimp.

Nitrifying (bacteria) Process of converting ammonia to nitrite and nitrate.

Nitrobacter Bacteria that convert nitrite into nitrate.

Nitrosomonas Bacteria that convert ammonia into nitrite.

Operculum External covering to the gills.

Osmoregulation Method by which fish regulates its internal salt content against that of the surrounding water.

Ovipositor Tube for depositing eggs, which is extended at breeding times by the female of some egglaying fishes (Cichlids and the Bitterling, a freshwater Cyprinid).

Peat Material often used as a filter medium (to acidify the aquarium water), or as a base covering for the benefit of those Killifishes which bury their eggs during spawning. May also be used by aquarists to enrich the gravel for improved plant growth.

Pectoral (fin) Paired fins immediately behind the fish's gills.

Pelvic (fin) Paired fins on the fish's ventral surface, ahead of the anal fin. Also known as the ventral fins.

pH Unit of measurement of the aquarium water's acidity or alkalinity. Freshwater aquarium: pH 6.5–7.5. Marine aquarium: pH 7.9–8.3.

Pharyngeal (teeth) Teeth located in the throat (of Cyprinid fishes).

Photosynthesis Process by which green plants, under illumination, utilize carbon dioxide and nutrients to build sugars and starches within the green cells, and give off excess oxygen.

Power filter Filter unit powered by means of a small electrically-driven water pump as opposed to being air-driven.

Protein skimmer Device for removing organic matter from the water in marine aquariums.

Quarantine The isolation of new fishes (and plants) in case of disease before adding them to the main aquarium collection.

Rays Spines supporting the tissues of the fins.

Reflector The hood of the aquarium containing light fittings.

Root Feeding system of plants. May be anchored in the aquarium gravel or, in the case of floating plants, just trail in the water.

Runners Young plants sent out from an established plant; may be removed and re-rooted elsewhere to form a separate plant.

Salt Sodium chloride (NaCl). May be used as a prophylactic bath for freshwater species (use only natural sea salt).

Salt mix Any proprietary brand of chemicals which, when mixed with freshwater, produces artificial seawater suitable for use in the marine aquarium.

Scales Thin bony plates covering the skin of the fish.

Scutes Thick, armoured plates, instead of scales, found in Catfishes.

Sealant Modern, non-toxic, silicone-based adhesive used in construction of all-glass aquaria and for repairing leaks.

Shimmying Stationary, weaving motion exhibited by chilled fishes.

Shoal Collection of one species of fish swimming together as a group.

Siphon (tube) A method of transferring liquid automatically from a higher level to a lower.

Soft (water) Water containing few dissolved minerals.

Spawning The act of reproduction.

Spawning tank A separate aquarium especially prepared for the purpose of housing a breeding pair (or shoal) of adult fish and where the young fry may be raised.

Species Classification term used to denote allied groups of fishes within a genus.

Strain Aquarium-developed variant of a species, i.e, long-finned, albino, coloured differently from the natural form.

Stripping (handstripping) A manual process of removing eggs from a female fish and of the milt from a male fish. Usually practised in Fancy Goldfish culture.

Substrate The bottom covering of the aquarium base.

Swim-bladder Organ inside the fish's body which automatically adjusts its buoyancy in the water.

Tail The caudal fin.

Territory Area of the aquarium adopted by a fish as its own.

Thermometer Device for measuring the temperature of the aquarium water.

Thermostat An electro-mechanical (or electronic) device for automatically controlling the aquarium heater.

Tropical Describes species of fishes requiring heated water.

Tubercles Small white pimples that develop on the gill covers of male Goldfishes during the breeding season.

Tubifex Small red worms found in the mud of freshwater rivers. Used as live food for fishes.

Undergravel filter System of filtration using the aquarium gravel as a bacterial bed. Also referred to as a biological filter.

Variety Fish of the same species, in which the colour patterns or finnage have been developed and stabilized by selective breeding programmes, or that may exist in nature as local variants.

Ventral (fin) See **Pelvic; Fin.**

Water Flea See **Daphnia.**

Water turnover Rate (in litres or gallons per hour) at which the aquarium water flows through a filtration system.

Wattage Measurement of electrical power consumption, but generally used as an indication of a lamp's brightness.

White Spot (*Ichthyophthiriasis*) Highly infectious aquarium fish disease; the common name describes the symptoms exactly.

Worms Excellent food for fishes. Worms of all sizes may be collected (Earthworms) or cultured (Microworms, Grindal-worms and White-worms) to suit almost every size of fish from fry to adult.

index

teach® yourself

From Advanced Sudoku to Zulu, you'll find everything you need in the **teach yourself** range, in books, on CD and on DVD.

Visit **www.teachyourself.co.uk** for more details.

Advanced Sudoku & Kakuro
Afrikaans
Alexander Technique
Algebra
Ancient Greek
Applied Psychology
Arabic
Aromatherapy
Art History
Astrology
Astronomy
AutoCAD 2004
AutoCAD 2007
Ayurveda
Baby Massage and Yoga
Baby Signing
Baby Sleep
Bach Flower Remedies
Backgammon
Ballroom Dancing
Basic Accounting
Basic Computer Skills
Basic Mathematics
Beauty
Beekeeping
Beginner's Arabic Script
Beginner's Chinese
Beginner's Chinese Script

Beginner's Dutch
Beginner's French
Beginner's German
Beginner's Greek
Beginner's Greek Script
Beginner's Hindi
Beginner's Italian
Beginner's Japanese
Beginner's Japanese Script
Beginner's Latin
Beginner's Portuguese
Beginner's Russian
Beginner's Russian Script
Beginner's Spanish
Beginner's Turkish
Beginner's Urdu Script
Bengali
Better Bridge
Better Chess
Better Driving
Better Handwriting
Biblical Hebrew
Biology
Birdwatching
Blogging
Body Language
Book Keeping
Brazilian Portuguese

Bridge	Dog Training
Buddhism	Drawing
Bulgarian	Dream Interpretation
Business Chinese	Dutch
Business French	Dutch Conversation
Business Japanese	Dutch Dictionary
Business Plans	Dutch Grammar
Business Spanish	Eastern Philosophy
Business Studies	Electronics
Buying a Home in France	English as a Foreign Language
Buying a Home in Italy	English for International
Buying a Home in Portugal	Business
Buying a Home in Spain	English Grammar
C++	English Grammar as a Foreign
Calculus	Language
Calligraphy	English Vocabulary
Cantonese	Entrepreneurship
Car Buying and Maintenance	Estonian
Card Games	Ethics
Catalan	Excel 2003
Chess	Feng Shui
Chi Kung	Film Making
Chinese Medicine	Film Studies
Chinese	Finance for Non-Financial
Christianity	Managers
Classical Music	Finnish
Coaching	Fitness
Collecting	Flash 8
Computing for the Over 50s	Flash MX
Consulting	Flexible Working
Copywriting	Flirting
Correct English	Flower Arranging
Counselling	Franchising
Creative Writing	French
Cricket	French Conversation
Croatian	French Dictionary
Crystal Healing	French Grammar
CVs	French Phrasebook
Czech	French Starter Kit
Danish	French Verbs
Decluttering	French Vocabulary
Desktop Publishing	Freud
Detox	Gaelic
Digital Photography	Gardening
Digital Video & PC Editing	Genetics

Geology
German
German Conversation
German Grammar
German Phrasebook
German Verbs
German Vocabulary
Globalization
Go
Golf
Good Study Skills
Great Sex
Greek
Greek Conversation
Greek Phrasebook
Growing Your Business
Guitar
Gulf Arabic
Hand Reflexology
Hausa
Herbal Medicine
Hieroglyphics
Hindi
Hinduism
Home PC Maintenance and
  Networking
How to DJ
How to Run a Marathon
How to Win at Casino Games
How to Win at Horse Racing
How to Win at Online Gambling
How To Win At Poker
How to Write A Blockbuster
Human Anatomy & Physiology
Hungarian
Icelandic
Improve Your French
Improve Your German
Improve Your Italian
Improve Your Spanish
Improving your Employability
Indian Head Massage
Indonesian
Instant French
Instant German
Instant Greek

Instant Italian
Instant Japanese
Instant Portuguese
Instant Russian
Instant Spanish
Irish
Irish Conversation
Irish Grammar
Islam
Italian
Italian Conversation
Italian Grammar
Italian Phrasebook
Italian Starter Kit
Italian Verbs
Italian Vocabulary
Japanese
Japanese Conversation
Java
JavaScript
Jazz
Jewellery Making
Judaism
Jung
Keeping a Rabbit
Keeping Aquarium Fish
Keeping Pigs
Keeping Poultry
Knitting
Korean
Latin American Spanish
Latin
Latin Dictionary
Latin Grammar
Latvian
Letter Writing Skills
Life at 50: For Men
Life at 50: For Women
Life Coaching
Linguistics
LINUX
Lithuanian
Magic
Mahjong
Malay
Managing Stress

Managing Your Own Career	Pilates
Mandarin Chinese Conversation	Planning Your Wedding
Marketing	Polish
Marx	Polish Conversation
Massage	Politics
Mathematics	Portuguese
Meditation	Portuguese Conversation
Modern China	Portuguese Grammar
Modern Hebrew	Portuguese Phrasebook
Modern Persian	Postmodernism
Mosaics	Pottery
Music Theory	PowerPoint 2003
Mussolini's Italy	PR
Nazi Germany	Project Management
Negotiating	Psychology
Nepali	Quick Fix French Grammar
New Testament Greek	Quick Fix German Grammar
NLP	Quick Fix Italian Grammar
Norwegian	Quick Fix Spanish Grammar
Norwegian Conversation	Quick Fix: Access 2002
Old English	Quick Fix: Excel 2000
One-Day French	Quick Fix: Excel 2002
One-Day French - the DVD	Quick Fix: HTML
One-Day German	Quick Fix: Windows XP
One-Day Greek	Quick Fix: Word
One-Day Italian	Quilting
One-Day Portuguese	Recruitment
One-Day Spanish	Reflexology
One-Day Spanish - the DVD	Reiki
Origami	Relaxation
Owning a Cat	Retaining Staff
Owning A Horse	Romanian
Panjabi	Running Your Own Business
PC Networking for Small Businesses	Russian
	Russian Conversation
Personal Safety and Self Defence	Russian Grammar
	Sage Line 50
Philosophy	Sanskrit
Philosophy of Mind	Screenwriting
Philosophy of Religion	Serbian
Photography	Setting Up A Small Business
Photoshop	Shorthand Pitman 2000
PHP with MySQL	Sikhism
Physics	Singing
Piano	Slovene

Small Business Accounting
Small Business Health Check
Songwriting
Spanish
Spanish Conversation
Spanish Dictionary
Spanish Grammar
Spanish Phrasebook
Spanish Starter Kit
Spanish Verbs
Spanish Vocabulary
Speaking On Special Occasions
Speed Reading
Stalin's Russia
Stand Up Comedy
Statistics
Stop Smoking
Sudoku
Swahili
Swahili Dictionary
Swedish
Swedish Conversation
Tagalog
Tai Chi
Tantric Sex
Tap Dancing
Teaching English as a Foreign
  Language
Teams & Team Working
Thai
The British Empire
The British Monarchy from
  Henry VIII
The Cold War
The First World War
The History of Ireland
The Internet
The Kama Sutra
The Middle East Since 1945
The Second World War
Theatre
Time Management
Tracing Your Family History
Training
Travel Writing

Trigonometry
Turkish
Turkish Conversation
Twentieth Century USA
Typing
Ukrainian
Understanding Tax for Small
  Businesses
Understanding Terrorism
Urdu
Vietnamese
Visual Basic
Volcanoes
Watercolour Painting
Weight Control through Diet &
  Exercise
Welsh
Welsh Dictionary
Welsh Grammar
Wills & Probate
Windows XP
Wine Tasting
Winning at Job Interviews
Word 2003
World Cultures: China
World Cultures: England
World Cultures: Germany
World Cultures: Italy
World Cultures: Japan
World Cultures: Portugal
World Cultures: Russia
World Cultures: Spain
World Cultures: Wales
World Faiths
Writing a Novel
Writing Crime Fiction
Writing for Children
Writing for Magazines
Writing Poetry
Xhosa
Yiddish
Yoga
Zen
Zulu